People and Places Across Canada

David Gidmark's perceptive, light-hearted account of his adventures and observations as he bicycled across Canada from coast to coast includes a host of sights, sounds, and colourful characters. And then there's the innkeeper's daughter . . .

"She had short cropped black hair, light-coloured features and dreamy, faraway eyes. She was tall, five feet eight inches I would guess, and this added to her classic appearance.

"I made a move. She was getting off at eight and yes, she wouldn't mind doing something after that.

"We went swimming at a lake nearby and the evening progressed from there . . ."

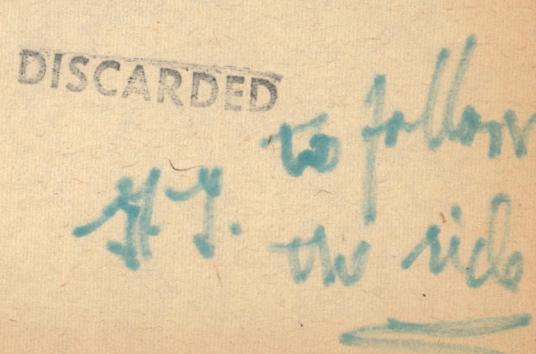

JOURNEY ACROSS
A
CONTINENT

by David Gidmark

PaperJacks LTD.

MARKHAM, ONTARIO

L3R 2M1

An original Canadian book
first published by

PaperJacks LTD.

JOURNEY ACROSS A CONTINENT

Original PaperJacks edition published March, 1977

No part of this book may be reproduced or transmitted in any form by any means, electronic or mechanical, including photography, recording, or any information storage and retrieval system, without permission in writing from the publisher.

© 1977 by David Gidmark

Cover illustration by Valerie Fulford

ISBN 0-7701-0008-2

All rights reserved

Printed in Canada

This original PaperJacks edition is published by

>PaperJacks Ltd.
>330 Steelcase Road East
>Markham, Ontario L3R 2M1
>Canada

To Vernon and Irene Gidmark
for extraordinary loyalty

Chapter 1

I went from Québec to British Columbia to cross this continent by bicycle.

This is a vast land, Canada, and I wanted to know it better, to really feel it, to breathe its dust and suffer under its sun. To withstand its wind and rain. I wanted to feel every one of the miles that separate its west coast from its east coast and to earn this insight I hoped to gain. What good to travel in a car and be closed off from the smells of this land, separated from Nature by Plexiglass and reinforced steel?

You could do this trip in a camper or in a mini-bus but why not feel the nights and feel the sun and the wind? The voyageurs used to do it by canoe over great routes of lakes and portages that stretched over thousands of miles.

In the centennial year, 1967, a group travelled by canoe from Rocky Mountain House near the Canadian Rockies in Alberta to Montréal. It must have been a hard trip but apparently they arrived all right.

In 1956 in the United States, four men went from Denver, Colorado to Old Town, Maine by canoe, passing down the North Platte and Missouri rivers, up the Mississippi River and its tributaries and into Lake Superior and across the Great Lakes along the old fur trading routes to Montréal.

One hundred years before that, in 1856, the adventurer Robert Campbell left his post with the Hudson Bay Company in the Yukon Territory and walked all the way to Montréal on snowshoes. That was a distance of three thousand miles and he did it through the winter.

Any self-propelled trip the nature of these almost assures you an intimate knowledge of the country.

Chapter 2

There aren't really many roads to choose from in crossing Canada, at least not many roads that go the entire distance. In fact, the Trans-Canada highway is really the only one that goes all the way from British Columbia to Newfoundland. But this is a heavily-travelled route in the summertime. Tourists from the United States clog the transcontinental ribbon along with hordes of Canadians. And hitch-hikers are lined up rucksack to rucksack all along the way. The Trans-Canada highway is the main route — the cheapest for them — from Vancouver to Toronto and Montréal. From eastern urban centre to western urban centre with rarely a stop to see and to sense their wonderful country along the way.

This little thread of concrete unites the east and the west. It is mind-boggling to stand on it out in Alberta or Saskatchewan or Ontario when there is no traffic and to think that it is only this which unites the great cities of the country. Quite unlike the United States where the Interstate highways have automated travel so much that you may one day be able to put the car on automatic pilot. But is this truly the kind of travel that will allow you to learn and to feel? It's like taking a plane to Europe. How ludicrous it is to see people on the bum, hitchhiking and staying in youth hostels, who begin these impecunious journeys by taking multi-million dollar machines which travel at nearly seven hundred miles an hour. And served by stewardesses, the models-next-door with atrophied smiles on their faces. It's more like teleportation.

Why not the infinitely more romantic way to go — ships? Why not the smell of the sea instead of the stewardess' Chanel No. 5 from her last run to Paris? Why not the good and plentiful grub of a merchant ship instead of the pre-prepared, insufficient and appeasing fare of a commercial airliner? Every man needs to see Europe, but does he really need to get there in five hours?

Getting to Europe to bum around and going there by plane is like hitching from Montréal to California and having your chauffeur drive you to Cleveland. The romance is gone. The feel belongs in travel. One doesn't travel to send postcards. We don't travel to "place-drop" when we get back.

"I travel not to go anywhere, but to go. I travel for travel's sake. The great affair is to move." That's what Robert Louis Stevenson had to say about it. Can you see him being served chewy chicken and processed peas aboard a Pan-American flight?

He would have taken a sailboat, probably, even today. He would have admired Sir Francis Chichester who sailed around the world in Gypsy Moth when he was past sixty. He would have given a good slap on the back to Robin Graham, the gutsy kid who left Los Angeles harbour in the Dove when he was sixteen and came back five years later, introduced to manhood by the sea. He would have shaken the hand of Robert Manry, the Cleveland newspaperman who left his office and Middle America behind in 1965 and took the fourteen-foot Tinkerbelle from Plymouth, Massachusetts to Plymouth, England.

I can't remember who said that a man must live before he dies but he had it right. And this is part of it. Doing it before it's too late. Why stagnate when you can be out on the road and have the juices running? Why breathe the pollution of the city when the air is magic out there?

There is also the challenge involved in setting yourself a goal. A goal that may be seemingly unattainable — in this case, a continent. And to have conquered this land by hard work, endurance and, most of all, force of will. This matter of will is no insignificant obstacle. In fact, it may just be the only serious obstacle. Sitting in a comfortable chair planning something like this, one may think that anyone with two strong legs can make the trip. Actually, anyone with two legs (or maybe less) could do it. The motive power is not the legs but the will. Many people have the strength to climb mountains; few have the courage. And so it is with a trans-continental bicycle trip or a solo, trans-oceanic voyage in a sailboat. These demand a consummate will. Not to give up when your viscera are spilling or the tops of your thighs are burning. Not to stop when the thought of many 100-mile days faces you in the morning.

This is not a new experience for me. In fact, I started this same trip ten years ago. And failed. Two of us tried it, my friend Nile Ostenso was my companion in that truncated version.

We were young then, in our late teens, and full of enthusiasm. The idea was the same then as now; to cross the country.

We shipped our bicycles out west to a point not far from Vancouver and we hitch-hiked out to them. Unfortunately, the railroad was late in delivery and we had to wait more than a week for the bikes to arrive. Fickle as we were, this already began to wear on our enthusiasm. A night we spent in back of the train station was the worst of the whole trip.

Not having money to put ourselves up in the town anywhere, we lay the sleeping bags down in some old lumber not far from the station. We weren't far from the sea at this point and everything was damp. Waking the next morning, I found that a huge two-inch slug had crawled in my hair during the night and every bit of tossing and turning I did during that night only served to spread more of everything that poor slug owned all through my hair.

Well, we finally got the long-delayed bicycles and started off. We went up the Fraser River Canyon and, much to our surprise, a hot sun and 103-degree heat made the going excruciating. What was this desert heat doing in British Columbia! Water was everything to us. We ate almost nothing but drank continuously, until we were nearly bloated each time we stopped for water.

The Fraser River was magnificent. Roiling and mad, it almost seemed as if it were being fed from the spring run-off, although it was mid-July. On the other hand, that may well have been the case; a couple of days later we saw snow alongside the road in Rogers Pass.

It was hard to imagine how canoeists manage the Fraser, although there are some who do. We rose and descended along the river, now close to it where the road sunk into a valley that met the river, now high above it as the river cut its way through yawning gorges. Each of the ups meant a lot of walking for us. The 100-degree heat clung to the skin like warm underwear in winter. Profuse sweating was the only thing that kept us from fainting.

A river as big as the Fraser must have good fishing, we assumed; this was Canada after all, was it not? So we rigged up a line and a sinker in an enthusiastic effort to augment our diet. We found an eddy in the Fraser and tried our luck. For hours that afternoon we eagerly awaited results but our enthusiasm went unrewarded. Little respites like these gave us needed change from the monotonous churning of the bicycle pedals.

There's an aerial ferry in the lower part of the Fraser River Canyon. We wanted to take it but for some reason did not. Fear may have played a part. It can carry one vehicle and several people. It's harrowing though. The conveyance, like a cage, is suspended from cables more than one hundred feet above the river.

Leaving the Fraser and going northeast into the Thompson River Valley, we rode into the desert of British Columbia. We were used to thinking of British Columbia as a place of constant rain, certainly in the winter. But this isn't true of the interior. The coastal mountains stop the greatest part of the moisture coming in from the Pacific. And here in the Thompson River Valley, vegetation was sparse and it resembled a desert. And any relieving wind that we felt in the Fraser River Canyon was gone now — nothing left but an unrelenting heat. We were taking British Columbia the hard way, in 100-degree heat over hills that were three, four, five and sometimes more miles long. The heat was so onerous that we rode late into the night hoping this way to avoid the heat of mid-day.

In Revelstoke we entered the beautiful Selkirks, mountains so impassable that a serviceable road — the final section of the Trans-Canada highway — was completed only three years before in 1962. Before that there was a dirt road, called the Big Bend highway, but that was treacherous. It is another measure of how truly big and young a country Canada is to think that Canada could only be crossed, with any degree of convenience, in 1962. It was also in this area that the Canadian Pacific drove the last spike which completed Canada's transcontinental railroad in the 1880's. Eighty years between the completion of the railroad and the opening of the highway! Prior to the finishing of the railroad, travellers had to go to the United States in order to get to Vancouver.

We thought the Rogers Pass between Revelstoke and Golden might be a nearly insurmountable barrier, having heard stories of winter snowfalls of four feet and death-dealing avalanches. Fortunately, as I remember it now, the task wasn't all that formidable. It looks hard at first to go though the Rocky Mountains, but it isn't really. (I may soon kick myself for this). These mountain ascents are often fairly gradual, following a river or a pass. It can be rougher in glaciated area like Ontario, Québec and the Midwestern states where there's a hill a minute.

I don't remember any great hills going up to Rogers Pass but there was a blockbuster coming down. We must have coasted, at fifty miles an hour, for eight miles. Practically speaking, we may have had to walk all that had we been coming from the other direction.

The pass was breath-taking; gigantic firs and shear rock escarpments met the road. The air was cool at this altitude, a relief from the oppressive heat of the Thompson and Fraser valleys. From the 100-degree heat of a couple of days before, we were now so high that snow covered the shaded spots of the forest floor.

We rode into Golden on the eastern slope of the pass. It was late. Up until then, our nights had been mercifully free of mosquitoes. We had no tent and the only thing standing between us and the little nemesis was fresh air and wishful thinking. These no longer did the job.

The mosquitoes were unrelenting. We looked around the little town of Golden and couldn't find an area that was cleared off enough to keep mosquitoes away. We tried one place but it didn't work. Climbing in our sleeping bags and folding the bags inward on us was unworkable. The heat — it was still 80° outside — was insufferable.

Tired and discontent, we picked up our things and once more made a trip around town, locating finally a promising area on the edge of some buildings. It was a little lot, dirtier than hell, but it proved to be free of mosquitoes, and therefore suited to our needs. Happy to be able to spend an untormented night, we fell quickly asleep. Great was our surprise the next morning when, waking to find the bikes, bags and ourselves surrounded by cars, we saw we had camped in the middle of a parking lot.

The next obstacle east of Golden, save for some ordinary ups and downs, was the continental divide. The Trans-Canada highway crosses the continental divide in Kicking Horse Pass.

On the western slope of the pass, we had an interesting opportunity for a little photography. We saw a black bear rummaging through some trash in a gravel pit. We were both convinced that a picture of one of us along side the bear would make a good souvenir. And we were both trying to convince the other that he should be the one to have his portrait taken with the bear. We didn't ask the bear, but some fairly logical reasoning (mine) suggested that Nile, because of his fleetness of foot and my familiarity with the camera, be the one to pose with the bear. Anyway, he got as close as prudence would allow and I got the picture, showing the ursine and the humanoid regarding each other with equal apprehension.

We reached the top of the pass after one of our frequent lengthy walks. Cutting off from the Trans-Canada highway on a road that went south through the woods, we came to Lake Louise. I think that if I had to say, offhand, the most beautiful place I've seen, it would have to be this beautiful, spectacular emerald lake, named after Princess Louise, Queen Victoria's daughter, which lies high up in the Canadian Rockies, surrounded by them and seemingly covered by them, so near do the mountains come to the lake's edge.

I once saw the lake on May 1st and even then it was covered by four feet of snow, the lake's striking beauty still overcoming the visitor.

There's a great hotel on the shores of Lake Louise, the Château Lake Louise, one of the old Canadian Pacific hotels. Of course it would be much better if this hotel were not here, and, although my instincts point this way, I can't help looking at the other side of the coin. It's hard to keep so many tourists from so much beauty. And after all, we are all tourists aren't we? Even the most pretentious among us. What if an assembly-line, plasticized Holiday Inn had been put up here? With perhaps a drive-in hamburger place next door? Tourists could be processed quickly and efficiently and wouldn't have to spend so much time contemplating the beauty of the place.

We rode down from the great elevation of Lake Louise to the highway.

This was to have been the most difficult part of our trip — the Rocky Mountains. But, as I mentioned earlier, our will hadn't been set and the remainder of the trip went the way of most dreams. We hadn't had much money to begin with — barely enough to get us that far, although we were getting by on a munificent $10 a week or something like that.

The week-long trip through the Canadian Rockies had left us truly exhausted. It's the physical fatigue that weighs so heavily on the mind. We were covering eighty to one hundred miles a day on the days we rode. This is never a good idea; the psyche begins to fear fatigue and it's difficult to appreciate the fact that the body becomes quickly conditioned to the work. But it is logical that the body should not be forced into such an immediate and strong test. We hadn't had the wisdom to begin gradually.

So we decided to quit. Sad word, isn't it? We went into Banff and slept the night behind a school. The next day we were walking around town when we met a truck driver who had come from Calgary with a load of groceries. He needed someone to help him unloading and wanted to know if we would be interested in helping him for a few dollars. We were.

To finish the story, we worked for the man that day and threw our bicycles into the back of the truck for the ride back to Calgary.

In Calgary, we packed up the bicycles and sent them home.

It was a good, strenuous trip across the Rockies. We didn't go farther east than Banff but we could at least take satisfaction in having done the hardest part.

Chapter 3

There had been other trips before; this trip across British Columbia was part of a progression of travels, often ones I took by bicycle but also on freight trains and by hitch-hiking.

It happened every spring, as you might guess, that tremendous attraction exerted by the horizon now that it was devoid of snow. It was a real fever that cried for appeasement.

At eleven I began by taking a bicycle trip to a town twelve miles from home. It seemed like an adventurous thing to do at the time. It gave rise to consternation in some quarters as my father nearly forbade me to make the trip, so risky did it seem to him. But it was done and there followed other longer ones. The next years there were many; the following years as well. And when I was fourteen I left home at 3:30 a.m. and bicycled to Lake Superior, one hundred and seventy-five miles away, arriving at 8:00 that evening.

Then came the freight trains and the hitch-hiking.

And now it seems the time is favourable for another try at Canada. I'm going to begin from the west again, this time in Victoria. There are prevailing westerlies on this continent and logic dictates that these should be at the back.

I've planned to satisfy my curiosity about a number of

things in this country. Therefore the itinerary will be a wandering one, not a direct route from Victoria to St. John's but rather one that will lend itself to freedom from a too-rigid route.

Another aim will be to avoid the large cities. The cities we have are for cars, not so much for bicycles or people. Taking a bicycle into one of these cities is not having as serious a consideration for one's safety as one should have. Maybe one day it will be easy to cross a large city by bicycle but it's not generally the case now. As cars lose their hold on people, cities will become more liveable. Urban mass transit is a necessary first step. As one hapless mayor said, everyone has a right to come downtown but he shouldn't have a right to bring four thousand pounds of steel with him.

I purposely did not outfit myself until I got to Victoria. There's no sense in shipping these things out there. It's just as smart to travel to British Columbia unencumbered.

The trip out was itself a long one. It was cold as I went from north to south through British Columbia, so cold that it snowed. If you live in Canada, you must like snow but snow in the third week of May can tire a soul already fatigued from the many long months of winter. For a time, I thought it would be good to begin as early in May as possible. I obviously did not have as good a conception of the western climate as I should have had.

The worst areas, of course, were in the mountains. For each thousand feet in altitude you simulate going north in latitude for a considerable distance. When I got to Vancouver, it was a reasonable and tolerable sixteen degrees.

Vancouver on a Sunday is a quiet city. The stores, and a goodly number of cafés and restaurants, are closed. Derelicts walk the streets of the old section, searching for a drink. Does Vancouver have more winos than any other Canadian city? I don't know. But until it is proven otherwise, the city has my vote. It must be the salubrious climate. The attitude of the people aside, the climate in the east and on the prairies doesn't allow for much malingering. The whole city steps briskly if the temperature is minus twenty degrees. But Vancouver is Canada's promised land, its California.

I tried to find a bicycle in Vancouver, on a Sunday. I decided to buy a used bicycle, a recycling that saves money and means having a bicycle whose character has already begun to develop. I picked up one of the local classified pages and was amazed to discover the number of ads for bicycles — fifteen or twenty of all makes and prices. Hope soon waned when I called ten or more numbers and found the bicycles had been sold within hours of the newspaper's hitting the stands. They were being snapped up like antiques at an auction.

Bicycling, in case there's anyone reading this who hasn't noticed, is a hot idea, a fad whose time is now. It wasn't the case ten years ago. A bicycle was the mark of the adolescent. You went through a limbo when you were too old to ride a bicycle and too young to drive a car. You may have been seen driving a car, but you didn't ride a bike to school for fear of being called some sort of oddball.

But now ride your bike to school if you like because it's in. Logic and good judgment don't really have much to do with the way people act. Logic and good judgment long ago would have dictated that our society adopt the bicycle as our major form of non-ambulatory transportation, instead of the poison-belching, cacaphonous motor vehicle. But then cars, hot and otherwise, were the thing. But as the good fads pass with the bad, this too shall pass — unfortunately.

There was nothing I could do about a bicycle in Vancouver on Sunday and, as the city was intimidating by its mere size — as so many are — I left that evening on the ferry for Victoria. But not before watching an interesting encounter in a restaurant.

It was a Chinese restaurant in the old section and I was there to have something to eat and to read a little. A down-and-out old-timer was sitting at the counter having some coffee and perhaps something else; I couldn't see well. He was an ugly sort by most standards, medium height with clothes that must have come from the Salvation Army draped over his back. He had a protrusive lower lip and a big nose. This was as funny to look at as it must have been inconvenient for him. When he chewed his face alternately folded and unfolded, or so it seemed. It looked as though he could have bitten an apple with his lower lip and nose.

He came into the restaurant without any money and this fact, as might be expected, made his exit rather tricky. By this time I was drinking coffee and watching everything over the top of the book I was reading.

He stood up and, as he was slow afoot, didn't quite make it through the door before the proprietor reached him. The owner was about fifty and wore a suit. Although it wasn't a big restaurant, the owner looked prosperous enough.

I couldn't hear what they were saying but the whole drama took place mostly in silence anyway. They both stood there in front of the cash register, the bum fumbling in his pockets for the non-existent money and the owner waiting patiently. The latter was watching the search with his hands clasped together in front of him and a mien that was a show in itself. He looked like he was at his mother's funeral. He wasn't angry — at least his face didn't suggest anger — but had instead a look of great sadness.

The bum fumbled first through one pants pocket and then the other. Then he rummaged through the pockets of his overcoat. And when this was finished, he began the same routine over, both of them lending a strange sort of seriousness to the whole thing by their continued participation in the farce.

It is not an exaggeration to say that this continued for more than twenty minutes. What either of them had to gain by this charade I couldn't see. I called over a waiter who was watching these two and told him to put the bum's bill on my own.

I was passing through Wisconsin some time ago and ran into a similar situation. While reading the news briefs in the paper, I came upon a piece telling of a man who was coming up for trial after having spent fifty days in jail. The charge was not being able to pay for a lunch at Kresge's. (I'm purposely not leaving out the name of the store.) The lunch was $1.86 and he had offered to pay for it by washing dishes. Kresge's, of course, isn't in the business of giving away free meals, nor is it an employment service. But anyone who would stand by and watch a man spend fifty days in jail for a $1.86 meal should spend that time in there himself.

Chapter 4

I left Vancouver Sunday evening on the ferry that goes to Victoria. It leaves from a point twenty or so miles south of Vancouver. The trip to Vancouver Island is short — about an hour on the ferry. It's a very lovely crossing; the ferry weaves in and out of the islands in the Georgia Strait. It felt, in the position in which I found myself, like the jet taxiing down the approach to the beginning of the runway. It is a slow twenty mile an hour loll to the runway and just as the turn is made the engines are opened up and the plane reaches several hundred miles an hour by the end of the take-off run.

The ferry trip over gave the same sensation although on my return run east there would be no attaining five hundred miles per hour; far from it. Maybe a healthy ten miles an hour. But there would be magnitude all right — five thousand miles of North America by bicycle, imposing in its own way.

I arrived at the ferry landing just north of Victoria in the early evening, itching to finish preparations for the start.

I bought a copy of the Victoria paper before starting off to town. I was a little apprehensive about it because of the futile search in the Vancouver paper through the myriad of advertisements for bicycles.

There were several advertisements and I called all of them. Only two bicycles were unsold. I felt myself in a race to get there with the others in the market place.

I thumbed a ride into Victoria with a man who was kind enough to take me to the first address I had. News of the trip I was going to make had evidently aroused this man's sympathy (or pity?).

The owner of the bicycle for sale turned out to be a compatriot; he and his wife came from Cap de la Madelaine, Québec and were in the Navy.

He offered a nice sales job on the bicycle. It was one year old and had only been ridden two weeks. It wasn't a bad bicycle but it looked a little like it had been dragged behind a car for two weeks. He had left it outside in all weather and it had rusted a little. It would take a little work before it could be totally reclaimed. Still, it wasn't a bad bicycle for eighty dollars. I told him the purpose of buying the bicycle and he suspected mental imbalance I'm sure. He offered to sell me an old car in the yard for the same price. He said it ran and would get me to Newfoundland much more easily than the bicycle. How well I knew. I told him I'd call in the morning if I decided in favour of buying it.

Left to find a place to stay in Victoria, I went to the youth hostel. It had been several years since I had stayed in one and they hadn't changed much, if this one was any measure.

It is a strange feeling to be in a hostel. Almost like one would feel with the same crowd over and over again in the Hilton hotels in Europe, given another time and economic stratum of course. There's a depressing sameness about it. The same jaded travellers and the same place-dropping.

There was a man there, an older fellow in his late fifties, who must actually have gotten his sustenance from the emotional reinforcement he found interjecting comments about his own travels in almost any conversation he was having. Rain in Victoria reminded him of the time it rained in Calcutta. The Victoria hostel charged $1.50 a night and the only ones he knew with the same rate were in Japan.

Monday morning held no more prospects for finding a bicycle than Sunday had. Making a deal with the displaced Québécois was the easiest way to resolve the situation. I called him up in the morning and went over to pick up the bike in the early afternoon.

Perhaps it is well here to describe the equipment on this trip, odyssey, fantasy or lunacy, or whatever you choose to call it.

First of all, as mentioned above, a good ten speed bicycle of solid and reasonably irreproachable reputation. And this one was used; sort of a recycling measure (no pun I hope). This is also in lieu of paying $150, $200 and even more for a new model. Thereby hangs a moral, hopefully. Ten-speed bicycles are generally over-sold. No one needs a ten-speed bicycle for riding around town. Ten-speed bicycles are for people who race with them. Anyone else would be well-suited to buy a three-speed or a five-speed bicycle and one with touring handlebars and a touring seat. If you're out for a Sunday ride you don't want to be watching the gravel shooting past nor do you want a bruised coccyx when you do sit up to get a look around. But advertising would have it that everyone and his sister needs a ten-speed racer. So the next time you see someone riding through town on a racer with his rear up in the air, his torso down and his cramped neck sticking up trying to see where he's going, think to yourself that this man, in terms of his needs, has been sold a lemon. Something good, efficient, and of quality can be superfluous, witness the nicely-bound sets of the world's greatest literature sold time after time to people who won't make use of them.

Obviously, a racing bike is indispensable for racing. Touring is another matter. Whether you need a racing bike for going several hundred miles overland at ten miles an hour is arguable.

At an average of ten miles an hour, I don't believe there is a great difference in wind resistance between a horizontal posture and an upright sitting attitude. And a touring seat with springs is a little more comfortable than the molded plastic racing seat.

Having taken the trouble to say all this, allow me to back up a little. This bike that I bought had racing bars and a racing seat when I bought it, so I'll give it a try, prepared to replace the two racing appliances with touring ones should it seem wise.

As I mentioned, this bicycle was in a state of near decrepitude. Rust was covering some of the nuts and bolts. The gear cables were loose and the tires were a little flat. (This whole idea may be a little flat.) Never mind, though, it gave the bicycle a lived-on look. There was a generator whose bulb needed replacing and a rather quaint squeeze horn that made a very insistent, baleful honk. I resolved to try it out on a cow.

For fifteen dollars I bought a good set of saddle bags, two compartments on the side — one on each — and a place on top for extra storage. Necessary gear for the bicycle included a wrench, tire patch kit and tire pump and undoubtedly many things that I forgot.

The saddlebags had a Canadian flag on them, which leads to an interesting reflection. In the United States, wearing an American flag on anything is out. In Canada, wearing a Canadian flag is à la mode. Not only that but it probably aids in the sale of any given piece of camping gear. Canadians are grateful of the chance to distinguish between Americans and themselves. Any opportunity to establish the difference is welcome. Hence the presence of so many Canadian flags on rucksacks from Turkey to Amsterdam. Canada must sell more flags per capita than any country of the Western world.

The whole affair proved to be a very colourful montage when put together; the bright purple frame of the bicycle, the brilliant red of the saddlebags and my pale white countenance as I contemplated the five thousand miles to St. John's, Newfoundland.

The Monday night before the big day was uneventful. Actually, I had planned on leaving quickly in the afternoon as I have no use for formal or anticipated departures. But I got lazy and allowed myself the luxury of a little procrastination.

I examined everything on the bike but still felt half-prepared. Maybe semi-preparedness is a little superstitious — you leave feeling that something will go wrong because you didn't give it enough attention and nothing does — hopefully. Minute attention to every detail bodes ill. I also got this far without having my head examined.

In other times for other ventures, I have often got the butterflies before setting out. Nothing serious, just a rapid flow of thoughts that races through the mind so fast that it impedes sleep. But there was nothing like that this time and I drifted off to sleep quickly.

I was up at 7:30 the next morning, not through any special willpower but because that was the rousing time at the hostel.

There wasn't much to prepare actually, just put the gear in the saddlebags and tie the sleeping bag and tent on top of that. There was no lock or chain on this whole assembly, by the way. The reason for the absence of the lock is not because I want to have this trip cut short by the disappearance of the bike. I simply don't like to lock things. Cars, houses and bikes are better off without locks. Come visit us in downtown Toronto, some of you are saying, and don't lock your car or your house there. Well, I'm afraid I would lock a few things in downtown Toronto, because I'm not a great believer in losing things either. But we should live in a society where we didn't have to lock things up. Simple-minded and Pollyanna you say? Maybe not entirely. There are areas where people would never think of locking their houses, where they have never locked bikes and where they leave their keys in the car so they will know where to find them. This freedom from paranoia is a blessed state. So if you find yourself getting uptight about locks, move to another, less-populated city. If you need a lock, you're too close to too many people. I lived in Montréal for a time and finally made what I consider to be a solid contribution to the social ecology of the city — I left it.

Bicycle locks, in common usage, are as recent as the bicycle fad of the last few years. And thefts grew apace, or perhaps faster, than the increase in bicycles. But it is a comfortable feeling not to have to lock a bicycle. So I'll travel across this country without a bicycle lock. (I may travel across without a bicycle!)

Part One

Chapter 5

I left Victoria and followed highway number one, the Trans-Canada highway, out of town. Some local people had suggested that I take a ferry that ran along the coast from Brentwood, just a few miles north of Victoria, to I forget where. Anyway the advantage to this was that it was to cut a very tough twenty miles from the trip to Nanaimo. This was a section of the highway that climbed from sea level to nearly twelve hundred feet above the coast. The suggestion offered a tempting shortcut but the trip was by bike and not by ferry so if there was a reasonable road over this pass, I felt obliged to take it.

Well, it was difficult. I had to go up several miles on foot because of the steep grade. The road was fine, though, one of those sections of the Trans-Canada highway with the paved shoulders. Walking always means a good change of pace from cycling; it's a chance to work out stiffness through a different leg action.

I thought to myself that it wouldn't do to forget to eat something in the morning. The only thing I had until noon was a great quantity of sunflower seeds. They don't work badly at helping to stave off an appetite and the salt is a must on hot days of bicycling. They all seem to be hot.

It was 16° when I left Victoria. Although this may seem cool and pleasant weather to ride in, a sweat works up quickly and off come the clothes.

I started off with long pants, a shirt and undershirt. The shirt came off quickly as the perspiration increased. The long pants lasted until the afternoon when I had a chance to change into shorts. The long pants were such an onus that it nearly felt as though there were no bearings in the wheels.

It was important, as far as I was concerned, not to try to ride too many miles the first day. For one thing, the initial part of the trip was the most difficult. The Malahat Drive, the mountainous section just north of Victoria, was a rude initiation to the east coast of Vancouver Island. Taking it easy the first day was supposed to reduce the soreness the second.

The bike appeared to be checking out all right. It ran well and the back tire was a little soft but wasn't losing any air. I should have been content with that. There were forty or fifty pounds of gear over that tire and most of my own weight as well.

In keeping with my plans to take it easy the first few days, I took a three hour break about mid-day after having covered that mountainous section and twenty-five miles of highway. I made a big helping of mushroom soup on the campstove I carried along. It may be an exaggeration to call it a campstove as it was only one burner, much like a Bunsen burner, and the fuel supply, a propane canister, was attached directly below the burner so that the whole apparatus was not more than a foot high. It was supported by four retractable braces that fell back to allow for setting the pot over the flame.

The stove is a quick heater and brings water to a boil fast.

The pots and pans, what there were of them, were all contained in a fold-up, canteen-like arrangement. They weren't too big nor too heavy but they served their purpose well.

Eating was never like this. It never is when you've been outside working. Each cell cries for energy and water. I gulped down the soup and a quart of milk as if I hadn't eaten for days. No one who eats food out of custom can realize what a great physical pleasure there is in it when one is desperate, or nearly so, for it. Once the immediate urge was sated, I topped off the meal with an apple and a good bunch of grapes.

And then came a little reading followed by a nap of an hour or two. I don't remember exactly how long the nap lasted but the whole stop took two or three pleasant hours. Needless to say, I carried no watch. It allowed for freedom from the clock.

The system was working well; I was not getting sore or tired too quickly. On another bike trip many years back, I travelled one hundred and fifty-two miles the first day — and paid for it later with sore muscles and a weak will to continue the next day. Too ambitious a beginning can dampen one's desire to continue.

Back riding again, I still felt good and rode easily until a few hours later in the evening when I stopped to have a couple of cans of sardines, not being ambitious enough to cook anything.

I continued on and, as it was just a couple of hours before sunset, began looking for a place to put the tent up for the night. It was a bit hard finding one. Either the forest was too thick or the cleared areas were farmers' fields (with the farmers not too far away).

I found an old, unused road leading away from the highway. It hadn't been used in so many years that the roadbed was covered with grass. The entrance to the road was sealed off by a barbed wire fence, so I had to take the sleeping bag and tent off the back of the bike, throw them over the fence, lift the bike over the fence and follow it myself.

The area seemed free of mosquitoes, luckily. Strange because it seemed more verdant and alive than the average forested area elsewhere.

I set up the tent, read for a short while and fell asleep just after sunset. I had covered fifty miles the first day and for getting the feet wet a little, that wasn't bad. Only five thousand miles to go.

It began to get light the next morning about five o'clock. I said that there was no watch or clock along on this journey; that is the way it should be. Part of taking off from a city is not having to key travel, eating and sleeping to the movements of a clock. The only times I saw the hour during the day were those occasions when I was in a store or when I noticed one while passing through a town.

Likewise, keeping too close track of mileage can be frustrating, especially if the schedule is hard to keep for some reason. In the beginning, things go slowly and any time when there are mountains or heavy traffic the going is slow. It takes time to add up mileage every few miles so the best way to travel, it seems, is to keep the head down and to forget as much as possible about time and miles. As long as the bicycle is on the right road, it is enough to push ahead.

It rained after daybreak and just before I got up. It was cause for some apprehension; heavy rain inevitably means a wet tent and that leads to a wet sleeping bag. That's one of the times when biking looks silly and a nice, gentlemanly train trip begins to appear a more reasonable mode of travel.

This rainfall was, fortunately, little more than a shower and I went back to sleep. I had been too chary about tiring myself too much. I slept a few more hours beyond daybreak. I thought it a good idea to work leaving time so that it was closer to dawn. This wasn't entirely a picnic, after all.

I wiped down the tent as well as I could with a rag and then rolled the tent up. The tent was still wet but there was nothing to be done about that — short of waiting a few hours while it dried in the sun.

The second day was the day of crossing to Vancouver on the ferry. I kind of hoped to do more miles than on the first day. The muscles were quite free of soreness and everything seemed in a generally good condition.

Traffic was heavy over the last twenty miles into Nanaimo. The tourist season had begun and there was also the usual complement of logging trucks. A rather narrowed road without paved shoulders was the only thing there was to handle this traffic and me. On roads like this, it became a game (and a dangerous one) to avoid traffic. You must keep the bicycle on the right six inches of the roadway and hope for the best. And it must be steady. Any jerky motion could cause a following car to swerve out into the oncoming lane of traffic. Sometimes when a large truck comes up from behind or when the traffic gets too bottled up, the only thing to do is to go off on the shoulder.

A shoulder, unless it's paved, is really no place to ride a bike. The heavy gravel and sand in places can cause the bicycle to stop. And continual travelling over gravel doesn't help the tires any.

To these problems is added that of the occasional driver who feels that roads were made for motorized vehicles only. He gives you a loud honk and a growl in his rear-view mirror that asks the question "What in the hell do you think you're doing with a bicycle on a public road?" Fortunately, these drivers are rather rare.

The only surcease available from the heavy onslaught of traffic on the way to Nanaimo were a couple of sections of highway under construction. Regular traffic was diverted onto detours and I, being on a bicycle, was permitted to travel over the paved, and now vacant, road which was being worked on. A welcomed relief.

There are flaggirls instead of flagmen on many of these jobs now. Someone has finally figured out that it doesn't take a 200-pound construction worker to hold a stop — slow sign. It's nice to see the girls. Their presence alone is sufficient to make me believe road improvement is taking place.

I felt sorry that I wasn't spending more time on Vancouver Island. It is a beautiful place. The most impressive things, probably, are the magnificent trees, the gigantic Douglas fir and spruce that grow in such profusion. One of these trees looks as though it could easily make a cord of wood by itself — and this might even be a gross understatement.

Nanaimo is a bustling little city on the Straits of Georgia just across from Vancouver. The mountains on the mainland are easily visible from there although the smog that inevitably creeps out from Vancouver obscures the lower elevations.

The ferry to the mainland at horseshoe bay was to take two hours. It is amazing the number of cars, trucks and buses one of these ships can hold. The total must certainly be upwards of fifty. Bicycles were put at the head of the automobile deck so that they could be first out on the other side.

The ferry ride was a good and needed break from cycling and afforded time to read and sleep a little. Weather was beautiful and sunshiny as it had been all morning.

On the ship I met another fellow who was bicycling, he from the northern part of Vancouver Island back to Simon Fraser University in Burnaby, near Vancouver, where he was a student. After exchanging explanations about each other's trip, we decided to ride together to Burnaby. His knowledge of traffic and roads around Vancouver was to help me a good deal.

Then began what was the worst part of the trip so far: the nerve-wracking weaving through the heavy traffic around Vancouver. The sun beat down and made it hot peddling. But the great irritant was the cars and the loud and continuous noise that went with them.

On the first section of the road into Vancouver, we

were on a four-lane highway with a paved shoulder. The shoulder was all right but this highway rose and fell over Burrard Inlet hundreds of feet at a time. And each rise meant a great hill that had to be negotiated on foot. Later I was to ride up more and more of the hills but in the beginning I was walking them in order not to leave the muscles feeling it too strongly the following day.

After that initial difficult stretch, it got worse. We were on roads with no shoulders for several miles. The four lanes of traffic streamed by, for the most part unmindful of us.

That whole crossing of Vancouver seemed to be just one stop and start after another. The loud, steady drone of the traffic kept our nerves on edge.

Finally, mercifully, it ended in Burnaby. The traffic grew lighter and the roads had better shoulders. My friend turned off and I continued on to the road that goes along the north shore of the Fraser River.

I checked the mileage for the day and was surprised to find, even with the torment of crossing Vancouver and the easy two-hour ferry ride that had come before, I had gone more miles than the first day. And I was beginning to feel in better shape.

The following day, Thursday, was a great improvement over the first two. It was sunny and mild and gone was the heavy traffic that had been so irritating the first two days.

I rose late and began from Haney along the north shore of the Fraser River. The highway there is a nicely-paved two-lane section called the Lougheed highway. It ran close to the river in many places. Above it mountains were beginning to rise to wall in the valley. There were the usual hills in this area but still it was not what could have been called mountain travel. That came after Hope.

When you're on a bike and you have been riding for many hours, it may easily seem much warmer than it is.

It was around 20° but it seemed like 30° or 35°. The cycling wasn't hard but I had been doing it all day under a hot sun. Fortunately, a welcomed surcease came in the guise of a lounge along the side of the road just east of Agassiz. I must have had four beers before sitting down, such was the thirst that demanded satisfaction. It was a good psychological respite as well; to be able to relax in cool, comfortable surroundings — with a little libation — does wonders for the psyche. In that blessed cool room with chilled beer I passed a contented two hours, first reading a little, then talking with some of the locals and finally playing some pool where I won enough for a little stake.

This lounge was full of surprises too. There, at five o'clock in the afternoon, a topless dancer came on a little stage to entertain the patrons. I might have beaten a hasty retreat but it would have served no purpose.

Leaving there, and doing my best to keep the bicycle from wobbling, I did a fast twenty-five miles to Hope in two hours. The notion of spending a night in the hotel there had tempted me. It would have been a good chance to wash up, take it easy and spend a night in a bed. Unfortunately, the places were either full or too expensive. But not being one to miss an opportunity, I rationalized that, in as much as I had been willing to accommodate the budget to allow for a night in a hotel, it would do as well, with the same money, to have a large supper, courtesy of my expanded budget. I went to a restaurant and ordered fried chicken and a host of other things probably best left out of a working-man's diet.

I left Hope the next morning without having had any food, save the few handfuls of raisins that I had been carrying along. This was to be the first taste of true mountain travel. And what an introduction it was. There must be a more descriptive word for it. Something that would combine shock, surprise and fatigue. I had been told that the road to Manning Park was uphill a good part of the way. Little was I prepared for what I found. The first hill just outside of Hope wasn't bad — perhaps two miles in length. Then there followed a stretch of reasonable ups and downs. Then it hit — a hill nine miles long. That's right, nine miles. It's pretty difficult to do anything on a hill this long but walk it. It was steep. With fifty pounds on the back of the bike, it's hard to go more than a quarter mile uphill without feeling near exhaustion. So I walked the whole thing and by that time I had passed the time by which I had hoped to cover the entire forty-two miles to Manning Park headquarters. I obviously was, in no small measure, underestimating mountain travel.

Walking becomes much more strained when there is a bicycle with fifty pounds of gear to pull along. About this time, the sunburn that had begun to develop the day before on my upper arms worsened. They were exposed to direct sunlight on this mountain for several hours. I did nothing about this condition but suffer it; my sunburns usually work themselves out after a day or two.

With almost no food, this continuous climbing was becoming very fatiguing. My walk was becoming weaker and weaker. Luckily, the beautiful and pristine mountains torrents kept me in a steady supply of pure, ice-cold water.

The munificent panorama of the mountains was another sustaining element. Sheer rock cliffs hung over the road in places. Waterfalls appeared here and there on the valley wall. I hadn't seen any wildlife for some time and was expecting to see at least a deer or two. Bear, grizzly and black, come down from the high mountain valleys in the spring to forage on the lower slopes. I hoped to see a bear; I had seen one, a black bear, crossing the road while I was on my way to Victoria before beginning the trip. The preference was, of course, to see one in the daytime so I could watch him at leisure. To hear one nosing around the tent in the middle of the night doesn't give a person much of a chance for observation — nor sleep. I wasn't too sure what bears ate, but I didn't want to be it. (I wasn't quite that worried). Bears don't attack as a rule, unless surprised or provoked. It is best to go carefully in an area where there are bears, because most of the problems with bears arise in surprise encounters, and only a fool would provoke a bear. The grizzlies weigh up to one thousand pounds and the blacks up to six hundred. They both run far faster than any human. Climbing a tree isn't always the good out legend would have it. Grizzlies aren't good tree climbers, but black bears can climb most trees. And surprising to many, taking your dog into bear country can be a very bad idea. Your Fido, even if a German shepherd, is no match for a bear. He won't frighten the bear but is likely to antagonize him. And when your dog finds his bravado ill-conceived, you know who he is going to run to for help — with six hundred pounds of angry bear on his tail.

When I reached the top of the nine-mile hill, it was almost a forgotten experience to ride again, having spent several hours pushing the bike during the ascent. It was almost five hours since I had started and still I had had no substantive food. The only chance of eating something was a little gas station at the top of the mountain. And their only larder was a rack of candy bars and gum. So it was to be that the whole forty-mile trip, up twenty miles on three hills, and over more than ten hours, had to be made on a handful of raisins and four or five candy bars. Rumor has it that sugar produces quick energy but I believe that the truth is that it furnishes a quick, short burst of energy and then results in a kind of lethargy so that the net result is negative. Nevertheless, it was food and left the stomach with something in it.

One of the local characters that so often people the hinterland stopped by. This was a smiling old-timer who drove up in a pick-up truck. The owners of the gas station, a couple in their mid-thirties I would say, took notice of his arrival with a chuckle.

This old codger had certainly passed his seventieth year. He wore what appeared to be a miner's helmet and three or four days' growth of beard graced his wizened cheeks. He walked with a stoop, his ever-present smile on his face. His whole wardrobe had the lived-in look for sure. Suspenders held up the baggy pants. And the pants were so commodious that it looked as though he could well have cached a week's grub in them. He evidently tried to minimize the effect of the changing seasons by wearing long johns during the summer. These latter rode substantially higher on the old-timer than did the suspender-held pants. Workboots completed the ensemble. He looked like he could tell a good tale or two of the back country.

The old-timer recounted that he had run into a bit of bad luck recently. He was building a good-sized log cabin in the woods and the roof fell in. He remained undaunted though.

It was a hot day and he needed a bottle of pop before pulling off. Unfortunately, he didn't have much more luck with the pop machine for a while than he was having with the log cabin. First he put his money in the bottle opener and turned the coin return button. They told him where the coin slot was. He fished the coin from the bottle opener and put it this time in the right slot. Then he turned the coin return and got his coin back.

"Durn thing!" he said, "All I wanted was a bottle of pop an' here I git my quarter back!"

The owner told him to put the quarter back in the slot and to open the door on the left. He put the coin in the slot, opened the little door and stood there.

"What do I do now?" he asked, fairly perplexed.

Pull out the bottle he wanted, they told him. This he did.

"Perty modern, these things, ain't they?" he said to me, surprised and amazed at how the thing worked.

After the man went out, the couple told of how the old-timer had hired two hippies to help him. This worried them because they were convinced that things would go to hell in the region. The unspoken assumption was, I guess, that red-necks are safe.

That stop was the half-way point in altitude between Hope and the Manning Park headquarters. There was quite a distance of moderate hills and riding again was a change and a relief. But it didn't last long. After a few miles I began the last climb, eight miles up to the park headquarters.

I was going up in altitude and as I did, and approached the snow, more and more of the beautiful flora of the region came into view. The beautiful alpine flowers that one sees only at this level stood out here and there. The pink wood betonies, the incarnadine Indian paintbrush and above all the cerulean lupine all offered themselves to the visual and olfactory senses.

Then there came a great burnt out region and gigantic charred tree trunks lay on the mountainsides, littering them like so many matchsticks.

During the climb up these two tremendous hills, there were a few people in trucks who offered lifts. One fellow even stopped a heavy dump truck on a steep grade to ask me. To all these people, I answered that I preferred to go it alone. They must have thought I was crazy. I thought I was.

Chapter 6

The long climb up to Manning Park headquarters finally ended. Forty-two miles had taken more than ten hours, an unusually long time.

Whoever runs the restaurant at the top of the park does a good job of it. I believe it's operated by the park service. After such a long, killing grind I looked forward to rewarding myself with a good meal and plenty to quench the thirst. The eternal thirst always demands satisfaction. I probably drank more water in a day than most people do in a week.

It was great sitting there in the restaurant. Food and drink, like anything else in life, has to be earned to be appreciated. And when it is, in this case ten hours on the road mostly uphill, its worth is magnified tenfold. Those who haven't starved or haven't worked don't know what food and drink are. I settled back over the meal and coffee and read Time magazine, a little savouring of luxury at the end of a day of heavy exercise.

There was a campsite two or three miles down from the park headquarters in the direction of Princeton. A little brisk moving got me there before dark.

The day had been blistering hot; it cooled off in the evening and at night, after midnight, it got biting cold. The altitude weighs heavily against a mild night. When this happens, every spare piece of clothing is pressed into action; long pants go on, socks go on the feet and the undershirt and long-sleeved shirt are doing their thing. I bunch up like a fetus in the sleeping bag and hope for warmer times. A trip outside in the middle of the night to answer Nature's call reveals the wealth of the diamond-like nocturnal sky. The constellation Lyra is the only one I recognize right away through the opening in the trees above. And Vega, alpha in Lyra, is shining bright with its bluish-white light, queen of this night's sky.

I fall into lazy habits in the morning. I have the first eye opened shortly after sunrise and note right away that it is still rather cold, too cold, I tell myself, to be riding a bike. So I roll over and go to sleep. Awakening a few hours later, I still notice a chill, perhaps only this time in my memory. Nevertheless, it is enough to send me to sleep for a little while more. And when I finally roll up the sleeping bag, and then read and write a little, it is nearly eleven o'clock. It's a little late to be starting, but lassitude doesn't allow anything else.

The western side of Manning Park was nearly all uphill. It was reasonable to assume that the eastern slope would be mostly down hill. That was what I was led to believe by some people who were supposed to have been familiar with the area. Unfortunately — and this I was to find many times — people who are used to driving over a road in a car just don't have a good sense of its topography. What is level to them can be a depressingly long hill to someone on a bike. One great hill along their whole route can impress itself in their minds and they remember the whole road as being hilly.

There were many downhill runs between Manning Park and Princeton, but not as many as there should have been. I had the strange impression that I was being shortchanged. Not long after starting I did something that I was to regret later; I took my T-shirt off during the worst heat of the day.

The beautiful, verdant mountains and the pure, fast-running streams on the west side of the mountain gave way to an arid country dappled with sagebrush punctuated here and there with a Ponderosa pine, a tree that is distinguished from other members of the pine family by its orangeish bark.

About this time, I had my first bear contact, albeit not too close a one. As I neared him, a large black bear was coming to the road as if to cross it. When he saw me, he turned and walked slowly back into the woods from where he had come. I continued, at a rather brisk pace, on down the road.

There were an uncharitable number of hills to be overcome on the way to Princeton and, during this time, my back was steadily becoming burnt and crisp, although it was actually difficult for me to tell the extent of the burn. A sunburn has a strange way of developing and reaching a critical stage after you get out of the sun. I put my shirt on hoping to avoid a sunburn not quite realizing that I hadn't done it in time.

Saturday night was a good excuse for renting a room in a small hotel in Princeton and taking it easy. The sunburn by this time was so bad that sleeping between those nice clean sheets was no pleasure. It was like trying to sleep in an oven. No one who hasn't experienced this can possibly fathom what it is. The whole body burns; it is impossible to sleep on your back — if that is where the burn is — and only barely possible to sleep on your stomach or one of the sides. Each movement sets off searing sheets of pain running along the body. The pain was so fierce that I was sweating.

Luckily able to get to sleep, I awoke the next morning to find the pain somewhat diminished. During all this time I was pampering myself, needless to say, and was having meals in restaurants.

While doing nothing useful around Princeton Sunday morning, June first, I managed to lose my camera. No apologies for my stupidity.

Between the mountainous terrain and getting up late, I hadn't been doing much in the way of miles. Starting early in the afternoon I made excellent time, travelling the forty-two miles to Keremos before supper time.

A rather intriguing sign greeted me at the door of a cafe there as I went in to have something cold to drink. It read: "Public Breast Feeding Not Allowed in this Restaurant." This aroused sentiments of the would-be Robin Hood in me, seeming at first glance to take a deprecating view of one of civilization's warmest customs. Having a kindly feeling in my heart for both children and breasts, I asked the middle-aged woman in charge the reason for the sign. There was never any hint of an argument, happily, as she explained that they had only two booths and a woman nursing would occupy a booth for an hour or more, to the exclusion of other customers. She herself had breast fed, she said. (I assured myself, visually, that she appeared quite capable.) The discussion soon ended very amicably and I left.

There was only time enough to leave town before it got dark.

I looked for a place to set up camp as I left town and rode through the fruit-bearing valley south of Keremos. There was orchard after orchard and fruit stands not yet opened that lined the road.

Some miles from town I passed a small house just next to the roadway. A sign on the garage advertised paintings for sale. A man was sitting on a bench in the yard watching the setting sun. I turned in and asked him if he knew a campsite in the area.

He was in his fifties and had a long black beard that was just turning grey. He wore shorts and shoes but no socks. His looks and conversation belied a good intelligence. I was eyed a little suspectly at first until the purpose of my trip, which he quite approved of, was explained.

He told me I was welcome to put my tent on his small

patch of lawn. The two dogs — tied, fortunately — which guarded his place, looked like they would be satisfied with nothing less than my blood.

The artist was an immigrant from Germany. He told of two smaller dogs he had had and what became of them. Someone, evidently feeling that this artist was some sort of an undesirable eccentric, had drowned one of the dogs in the pond next to the house and had hung the other dog's dead body over the doorway. This, and a few similar incidents, did not make this man too favourably inclined to the people of the area, whom he regarded as boors.

His paintings, of which he had several hundred it seemed, were quite good. They were impressionist landscapes for the most part and bore resemblence to some of the works of the Group of Seven.

This poor old artist lived in a tough world, for everyone was against him. People in the area were uncultured and didn't appreciate his work. Galleries were unapproachable and when they did take his work, they often forgot to pay. Canada didn't have the cultural awareness of the European countries nor the savoir-faire of the United States.

His modest house was a rain of oddments that he had collected over the years. His plumbing was outdoor and the cooking was done on a camping stove. Nevertheless, we had a couple of fine cups of tea in the evening and again in the morning when an unexpected rain got me up early.

This man's kindness was very much appreciated. I regret to inform you though, reader, that I paid dearly for the privilege of staying there. Paid by being riveted to a chair for hours on end listening to this gentleman expostulating on nearly everything. There was less chance of getting a word in the conversation than there would have been of getting Hitler in B'nai B'rith. I enjoy listening but not listening exclusively. Some people do not realize that one of the greatest impositions they can work on you is to force you to listen to them talk. No one ever learned anything while he was talking; therefore there are a fair number of ignorant, loquacious people in this world. How sad it is that an otherwise interesting, intelligent personality can be spoiled by verbosity. It doesn't matter what the person is speaking about; whether it's the weather, a bake sale or Einstein's Unified Field Theory. If he speaks too much he's an onus on his listener, that's all. Unfortunately, my dear artist friend fit this mold.

His hospitality was as effusive as his conversation. The latter nearly spoiled the effects of the former. But he was a man devoted to his work, which was creation, and these men are hard to find. He was a confirmed atheist, to his own profit and that of the church, he said. Among other things that he revealed about his past was the fact that he was a deserter from the German army in World War II and this certainly can be counted as an example of one of the most positive actions of the century.

Chapter 7

I left the artist with the kind heart and the loquacious disposition early that morning after the rain had stopped. This fellow had been very pleased about this part of British Columbia, the dry interior famous for fruit and hot summers, but to my mind, lacking a little in edification. The sage-covered slopes compared poorly to the lush mountains and fast-running, pure streams of many miles before. It resembled a desert. In fact, I believe there was a sign or two describing this as Canada's desert. They can have it, with apologies to all those who appreciate the stark, dry beauty of the desert.

That morning's downpour had given the first solid indication of rain that I had seen on the trip so far. Luckily, nothing materialized along that line; so much the better. This cyclist had to get across the country sooner or later and any extended rain could have held things up considerably. There isn't much to do in this sort of situation but to get wet. I felt that dragging plastic or rubber raingear along for protection would be more of a problem than an asset. All these things have to be stored and the saddlebags weren't as commodious as they might have been. So if it rained, I got soaked — period.

It was a quick twenty-five miles or so from Keremos to Osoyoos. I had been on the look-out for cherries, which I had been told were harvested first in Osoyoos during the year. No luck. I should have started this trip later. French-Canadians and Portuguese are among the ethnic groups that come into lower British Columbia to harvest the fruit crops in season. My artist friend had bemoaned the arrival of the Portuguese slightly, claiming that they come into the area, work like slaves, send for their relatives from Portugal (an old complaint) and then proceed to buy up orchards and businesses in the area.

Although it was a Monday, many of the stores in Osoyoos were closed. Rather than buying supplies, I was forced (?) to go to a beverage room where I sated an appetite and serious thirst with a hamburger and several glasses of beer.

I was anxious to pull out of Osoyoos because of the heat, although the idea was somewhat tempered by the tremendous mountain that awaited. And it was one of the most god-awful uphill climbs that I have ever seen — nearly sixteen miles. But the elevation at the end of the climb was so great that we (the bike and I) were once again returned to green mountain pastures and spruce and pine-covered hills. And the water from the creeks once again looked potable. Without these streams from which to draw water, the trip would have been very difficult. As long as the water in the water bottle is mostly clear, it's drinkable as far as I'm concerned. No reason to be fussy out here. I just dip the bottle in the creek, take one look to make sure that the thing is reasonably clear, and then down the hatch it goes. Then I fill the bottle for miles down the road when there may be no creek to resort to. Drinking from pure, cold water was one of the supreme pleasures of the trip because it so greatly satisfied the tremendous thirst that built up. Drinking may even have been more of a pleasure and a necessity than eating. Actually, the food intake seemed to be diminishing as the trip progressed. I began right away taking two meals a day and even those were getting smaller and smaller. And often in the morning I rose and began riding without having anything to eat, sometimes travelling thirty miles — which could take three to five hours depending on the terrain — before having had something to eat. The discipline was good for body and soul alike.

It was now great travelling; the Kettle Valley and the river that flowed through it were a verdant contrast to the arid territory of a day before. It also promised to be cold at night, a change from the previous evening's mild temperature in Keremos.

Just before a town called Midway, the mosquitoes began, the first real sign of them on the trip. It wouldn't be the last. Because of this new visitor, I sought out a clear spot on a hill overlooking the river. It was a spectacular place to pitch the tent. A mountain four or five thousand feet high was directly across the river. The tent site itself was several hundred feet above the river. Because of its prominence, I hoped that the lion's share of the mosquitoes would be blown away.

They weren't all kept away. And this incentive caused me to set up the tent with significantly greater haste than I had had before. The only thing that matches the unrelenting aggressiveness of these damn mosquitoes are the abominable black flies. Well, I didn't know if there were any black flies in British Columbia, but I wasn't going to wait to find out.

Back to the tent. It was an art to get the thing up and then get the gear ready and shove it in and jump in myself in the least possible time. Any delayed opening of the mosquito net was an open invitation for the beasts to infiltrate. Once inside, however, there were only two or three buzzing around and they met a swift demise.

I closed the flaps on the tent so that it was completely shut to drafts. If the tent is well closed, then a little heat can be built up from breathing during the night. It's a pretty cold proposition either way.

As there was some light left, I read a little before

turning in. I had begun moving around at six o'clock that morning and was eager to go to sleep.

Just as it began to get dark, I fell into a soft drowsiness. But just then there was a sharp noise outside the tent that gave me a start. Thinking it was only a branch snapping, I turned over and tried to sleep again. Then, there was a second sharp noise. Now I began to suspect a visitor, two-legged or four-legged. I listened. There were other noises, each time rather loud, as if whatever, or whoever, it was, had heavy steps. I looked out of the opening of the back flap in the direction of the noise. There was nothing. And slowly I lay down again, wondering why whatever it was didn't make an appearance. And then I heard it again! Was it a cow or a bear? A cow might have been grazing nearby. A bear might have been wandering through and have been too afraid to approach the tent. In any case, why were there these steps and no other noises that accompanied them, like growling or heavy breathing? You don't mind a prowler — a cow or bear or something of the sort — if you know what it is and where it is. But not knowing about something like this can keep you awake all night. There's always the chance that it could be some human or animal malefactor.

Then there was the noise again, and again. I jumped up and looked through the flap in the tent just in time to see the third Ponderosa pine cone falling to the ground.

It was only four miles from the little site where I camped to the town of Midway in the Kettle Valley. There was a little store there where I had the misfortune to pay 70¢ for a quart of milk. I should have asked if he had a monthly payment plan. Little stores, of course, charge more than big supermarkets; they have to. And stores miles away from commercial centres also have greater costs. But this fellow must have had two or three more escalation clauses to get that price up where it was.

Inflation has taken its toll all over. Everyone knows prices are going up but there are other, truly insidious practices going on at the same time. It's too bad the price of a candy bar goes to 20¢. But it's perfidious and deceitful if the size has been reduced at the same time. Not only has the price of this candy bar doubled, its size has shrunk by a third. The net weight is still marked, but who looks at the weight? And there's a greater ratio of paper-enclosed space to candy bar than before. Restaurants used to sell milk in small, medium and large glasses. Now, at greatly increased prices, it is sold in large and jumbo glasses, which are no larger than the original small and medium servings. But this poor storekeeper was to be exonerated, I guess. It was open season on tourists, wasn't it?

Grand Forks was the next major town along the way. I was ushered into the valley where Grand Forks lies by a long hill, perhaps the longest downhill so far. It must have been six or more miles in length. Perhaps I am naturally biased from my position, but a greater than reasonable share of the hills seemed to be uphill. In any case, this hill was an exception that kept me smiling for a long time.

This is the beginning of Doukhobor country. The first signs of this group that I saw were two large pink houses a quarter of a mile from the road. They stood like two massive sentinels on the side of a hill and were surrounded by more outbuildings than seemed to be needed by two families. The truth is that many more than two families lived in these houses; these were communes. Many of them dot the valley around Grand Forks, although most are now abandoned.

The sign one sees when approaching Grand Forks also announces a change. It had a welcome to the town by the churches and "religious groups." At the end of a list of Protestant and Catholic denominations was added "U.S.C.C. Orthodox Doukhobors." I wanted to find out more about these people and would have the chance to do so later, near Castlegar and Nelson.

Chapter 8

I didn't accomplish much in Grand Forks. These supposedly short stops had a way of turning into three- and four-hour layovers. Reading took a little of the time as did writing in this journal. I indulged myself to a great extent by loading up on avocados and canteloupe and then retiring to the city park for this vegetarian feast. Indulging oneself this way from time to time does as much for the spirit as for the body.

Walking through the town later, I ran into a man from out of town who asked a few questions about my destination and then invited me in for a beer at a nearby bar. Three beers later he was still going; I was trapped again. I must have the word "listener" written all over my face. Talkers zero in on me like mosquitoes on a sweaty arm. I find that it is a strangely creative time for me though. Their talk is so incessant and boring that all my faculties are free from any kind of attention and the imagination is able to go its own way.

This middle-aged gentleman resided in a western city and formerly had lived in Québec. That word was enough to start a long harangue and expose much of this man's feeling — or maybe one should say lack of it — toward the Québécois. It seems that this unfavourable attitude is not at all uncommon in the West. He claimed that Québec was receiving a disproportionate share of Federal revenues, that they had too many children and that Québec did not have enough esteem for the rest of Canada. He said that Québec should not be so worried about speaking French but should speak Canadian (English) like the rest of us. Then I was asked if I spoke gorf. After being unable to figure out what that was, he told me that it was frog spelled backwards.

Past Christina Lake east of Grand Forks, I ran into the two biggest hills, back to back, that I had seen so far. The second one was a downhill so it didn't work out badly. But it took me the better part of four hours to climb the grade up to Mitchener Pass. A tremendously fatiguing climb. But then, after a few miles of level road at the summit, came the pièce de résistance, twenty miles downhill to Castlegar. There was snow still on the ground and the air was cold. Before the beginning, I put on a heavy shirt. And then it was all downhill. There was a pretty little mountain lake named for Nancy Greene along the road. My hands became numb and my legs cold as the snow-covered forest flew by. That twenty miles took not much more than half an hour. A bicyclist's nirvana. I don't mean to complain and be ungrateful but there's a damn useless road at the bottom of this hill going into Castlegar. It's under construction, I guess; that is the only saving excuse. But this is a good place to separate the cars from the bikes. The bikes are the ones going through the chuck holes and riding through the heavy gravel. The cars are full of people gawking at the hapless biker.

Having heard that the Doukhobors in the area influenced the cuisine with their Russian specialties, my nose was on the prowl. I found my El Dorado at the Yale Hotel. They served the finest borsch accompanied by an incredibly tasty homemade bread. Borsch is a soup-like dish made principally of vegetables. A thick rich consistency is created by adding cream and butter. In the old days, Doukhobor women, often beautiful as young girls, got fat as tanks when they matured. Borsch is one of the reasons why. Now the Doukhobor women, with the assimilation taking place, eat less of the traditional fattening Russian dishes and pay close attention to their figures.

While ferreting around Castlegar I came upon a good find — a young Doukhobor girl, manager of a bookstore, who proved to be a well of information on the sect. That she was quite attractive added no little spice to the discussion and served to deepen my interest in the subject.

Doukhobor is synonymous, in a lot of Canadian minds, with nude protests, arson and bombings. But while the sect itself numbers over 15,000 adherents, perhaps as many as 20,000, it is the Sons of Freedom sub-group that is responsible for all the notoriety.

Sons of Freedom Doukhobors number about 1500, most of these living in Krestova, British Columbia. The rest of the Doukhobors, the great majority, are divided into Orthodox and Independent groups.

Doukhobors broke off from the Russian Orthodox Church at the end of the nineteenth century over their refusal to bear arms. So they came to Canada, not the first in a long line of draft resisters who came to the country that they felt offered the greatest personal freedom. Count Leo Tolstoy and the English Quakers supplied the funds that helped the Doukhobors to move to Saskatchewan where they were given free land. In 1908, they moved to central British Columbia after the government had required them to swear allegiance for the land they received.

It was around this time that the Sons of Freedom began to make a dubious reputation for themselves. The name Doukhobor means spirit wrestler in Russian. The Sons of Freedom evidently had a little more trouble wrestling with the spirits than did the rest of the sect.

Nudism became a tactic of rebellion for the Sons of Freedom. They stripped naked when they burned a building, when they had to appear in court or when they confronted the police. They even stripped during a campaign speech by John Diefenbaker, making it one of the most exciting speeches the conservative prime minister ever gave. Children were taught to strip to face up to civil authority. The young were taught to bomb and burn and often were sent by their parents to missions. And always with the justification that God wanted them to do it. If God wanted them to strip and burn, then He didn't take the time to get them out of jail. Sons of Freedom often spent many years in prison. In 1962, a young Sons of Freedom man died in prison after a hunger strike.

Peter Verigin, the leader responsible for leading the Doukhobors out of Russia, was killed in 1924 in a train explosion just east of Grand Forks. It is assumed by some that the Sons of Freedom were responsible for the murder. But could poor old Peter Verigin rest in peace? No. In the past fifty years his tomb had been bombed many times. It is now covered by reinforced concrete and surrounded by a garden.

The girl I was speaking to in Castlegar was an Orthodox Doukhobor. The Orthodox Doukhobors and the Independent Doukhobors don't bomb and burn and they tend to resent the guilt-by-association.

The Sons of Freedom have continued to this day to burn their own houses and public buildings when the spirit moves them. In fact, when I was there, they had just burned a community centre in Brilliant, the small village just north of Castlegar. They disrobed and watched the building burn. It was just like the good old days.

My lovely young friend called home for some more documentation while I went for supper. On my return, she had a list of reading material on the Doukhobors which she gave me. The material I was given was naturally rather favourable to the Orthodox Doukhobors, as might have been expected. It was plain to see from this girl's explanations that the Orthodox and Independent Doukhobors are rapidly being assimilated, if they aren't already. There is much evidence that the Doukhobors are almost through as a cultural entity: there is a great number of intermarriages between Doukhobors and non-Doukhobors. Traditional dress is no longer worn except on special occasions or for the tourist trade, and, perhaps most telling, Russian is rapidly disappearing as a language of communication. This generation seemed to be able to understand it although they did not use it. So it becomes plain to see that the Doukhobors, except for the feisty Sons of Freedom, are gone the way of so many other ethnic sub-groups. Not too much more than a memory and not greatly distinguishable from Mormons, Catholics or any of the other infra-societal religious groups. They changed quickly and drastically. From communal people who didn't even smoke or drink to ones who have become just part of the gang.

Anyway, back to the Doukhobor at hand. All of a sudden, in the course of the discussion, I found that her mother was in the shop, evidently having come over when I had left for supper. With my mistrustful mind, I readily assumed that the mother had come over to guard the daughter against wayward romantic inclinations. In truth, it seemed that she wanted only to explain the Doukhobors to this outside inquisitor. The mother wasn't able to add much except a reiteration that it was the fanatical Sons of Freedom who gave a bad name to the Doukhobors.

I had every intention of inviting the young Doukhobor lass (if they have lasses) for a coffee after her work was done, ostensibly to delve more deeply into Doukhobor history and traditions. Her mother was, regrettably, a dissuading factor. Such are the occasional disappointments of the road.

I wanted to catch a few of the spots important to the Doukhobors. To do this I had to go north toward Nelson. One of these places was Peter Verigin's tomb in Brilliant a couple of miles north of Castlegar. The other was the Sons of Freedom settlement in Krestova, several miles off the road to Nelson.

That evening was the first heavy rain I had encountered. I left Castlegar and was in the process of getting drenched as I wandered around outside the town, trying first one direction and then the other in my attempts to locate Brilliant. Brilliant, as it happens, is almost an appendage of Castlegar. I finally located it and the road that led up the mountain to Peter Verigin's tomb. It was still raining a little and promised to rain more. I had either to go back to Castlegar and get a hotel or to set up the tent out there hoping that it would stave off the rain sufficiently. I chose the latter and slept that night on the mountain where Peter Verigin is buried.

This tomb is a bit more significant than ordinary tombs not only because Peter Verigin, head of all the Doukhobors, is buried there but because the tomb itself has been a target of many Sons of Freedom blasts over the years. There was a bomb planted at the tomb shortly after the burial of Peter Verigin in 1924. Some say that his son, titular head of the sect after his father's death, had ordered the bombing to blow his father's remains sky high. It is difficult to say why the Sons of Freedom were so determined to bomb the tomb of Peter Verigin. He is as important to them as he is to the Orthodox Doukhobors. They seem to be willing to bomb only too readily. Whenever they feel moved by the spirits, or voices or whatever impels them, you'd better take cover.

The camping-in-the-rain operation was a success. It rained during the night but the sun came out early in the morning and dried the tent out before I got up. I got up so late that it had plenty of chance.

There isn't much in the way of the spectacular about Verigin's tomb. It is part way up the mountain overlooking the Columbia River and the valley where Castlegar lies. On a natural rock face in back of the tomb, an inscription in Russian and English portrays some of the attributes of Peter Verigin. The tomb itself is built, obviously, to be bomb-proof. It is a white cement block about twenty by twelve feet and two feet high. There are no niches on the tomb which could help a bomb gain leverage. A very difficult construction to bomb. The garden and tomb are surrounded by six-foot-high fence topped by barbed wire.

I continued up the valley toward Kootenay Lake. The turn off to Krestova, a place not on the map by the way, is at South Slocan. Each time I asked directions to Krestova along the way, I was asked why I wanted to go there. They apparently found it strange that an outsider knew of Krestova. The whole affair is rather mysterious. The Orthodox Doukhobors especially are suspicious of outsiders. Even though the Orthodox Doukhobors are fairly assimilated, they still adopt a protective stance vis-à-vis people from the outside.

I rode up the valley along a small road toward Krestova. There were no signs but continuous inquiries led me in the necessary direction. It was a great climb, as most of this trip had been.

It was a journey through the woods until I left them and came out on a high field filled with many shacks. It was a bizarre view. Thirty or forty clapboard shacks, several of which had been burned and others that looked like they should be burned. There was a strange silence around this village although it was mid-day. Actually there was little resemblance between this area and a village; the buildings were grouped together but not in the regular fashion, not arranged along a main road or on side lanes. Another striking feature was the general dilapidation that reigned. It was as if the houses and outbuildings had been put together with used lumber. There were few vehicles in evidence and no gas station or other store that you might have expected to see in a village of this size. The place was situated on a plain, part way up a mountain. It must have been an eerie display in days gone by when the Sons of Freedom set fire to their own houses on this mountain plain.

I looked hard for someone to speak to, but not seeing anyone readily at hand, I did not want to intrude on their privacy. And then I had visions of myself speeding away on a flaming bicycle.

A little beyond the older part of Krestova, there were some newer habitations and near one of these, three men were working on a basement. I pulled up to the house and asked the man nearest some directions. After a minute or two of talking, I asked him a few questions about Krestova. This put him immediately on the defensive. I was aware that Stefan Sorokin, putatory leader of the Sons of Freedom, returns from Uruguay in the summer to spend it among them and that there was a house in the area that he always used. I inquired of this man if he knew where Stefan Sorokin lived, and touched a raw nerve.

"Why do you want to know?" he demanded.

"Just curious," I answered, not too plausibly.

He said that he could not tell, that there were too many people who wanted to do harm to Stefan Sorokin. And he immediately launched in to a recapitulation of the directions out of the Krestova area, the supposed reason for the original inquiry. There was nothing to do but to move on.

I went off this mountain plain where Krestova lies and down into the Crescent Valley below, a little sorry at not having been able to speak to anyone at great length.

While going through a little corner of the valley on a dusty road, I came upon an old man working in a garden. I again asked for directions.

This man was a true peasant out of *Quite Flows the Don,* stooped from the waist and shoulders and with white hair and a white beard that danced up and down when he talked. His work was slow and methodical; shoveling stones out of the garden and then throwing and patting dirt back in place. Suspenders held up his pants. His high-backed shoes must have come from

Russia. He himself looked as if he had just come off the boat.

I helped him move a big, two-man rock from the garden and then had the licence, and privilege, to ask him some questions.

Was he a Son of Freedom?

"Ya," he answered in heavily-accented English.

Was he born in Russia?

"Ya," he said to this with all the taciturnity of the ages.

I asked him about Stefan Sorokin. He knew of him and where he stayed when he came to Krestova. But his English and my Russian weren't sufficient between them to make its location clear in my mind.

Would I like a cup of coffee, the old man wanted to know.

I welcomed the invitation, happy at this manifestation of openness on his part.

We walked into his house and I soon found that it was the dinner hour. He pulled a great jar filled with borsch from the refrigerator. He poured a hefty shot of this into a large sauce pan and put it on the stove to boil. While it was cooking, he had a chance to tell about his life.

He had six children and two were recently dead. Pictures of them lined the walls of his living room. A picture of John Verigin, present head of all the Doukhobors, and of Peter Verigin, were on display along with family photos. It was evident from the pictures of the family that, if the children had remained Doukhobors, they were probably no longer Sons of Freedom.

This man was 83 years old. He had come over with the first Doukhobors in 1898. He had met Leo Tolstoy. He remembered the day in 1928 when Peter Verigin was blown up in the train high in the mountains west of Castlegar.

He asked me what I knew of the Sons of Freedom and how I came to know it. I told him that it came from reading and from what the Orthodox Doukhobors had said. And what did they say, he wanted to know. I told him that I thought the Orthodox Doukhobors felt that the Sons of Freedom were a little wild because of the bombings and burnings that were often associated with them. He just laughed but said no more.

We didn't talk about much, really. I have the feeling that we were communicating more without it. In a few minutes the pan of borsch was ready. We ate this — several bowlfuls — with thick slices of buttered homemade bread and coffee.

I left him there in the garden, working away as he had for 70 years. The Sons of Freedom had seemed a little fanatical to me at first. I wasn't so ready to say that now.

Chapter 9

There isn't much to say about leaving the Castlegar area except that I had the feeling that I was leaving the mountains behind. Hills were now surmountable. I rode to Nelson, the city in the storybook setting on Kootenay Lake. Then along the west arm of Kootenay Lake for 20 miles to the ferry at Balfour. I had taken this route because of the reputed height of the Salmo pass east of Castlegar. If I never see another mountain pass, I'll live in peace and repose.

I caught one of the last ferries to Kootenay Bay that evening and found a spot for the tent that suited the needs of the moment perfectly. The rain that had been dogging my trail was threatening again. I found a supported roof that seemed to have once had a picnic table under it. It was made to order so it was there that I spent the night.

The next day was an uneventful one, except for being one of the most outstanding in terms of scenery. The road that followed Kootenay Lake down to Creston was basically level, almost like an eastern road, and this was a definite change, although it was littered with more than its share of small hills.

In Creston for supper, I indulged myself with a quart of milk, a watermelon and an avocado or two. There's no reward at the end of a long day's riding like being sated with whatever food suits the fancy.

From Creston, I assumed it would be easy to make Yaht, about 25 miles away, by evening. The road was well made and there was just the suggestion of a tail wind. The route followed a river upstream so this meant that the road rose as well. The grades were very mild and the shoulder was paved so that the going was very easy.

I was going along this stretch of highway when two men in a car pulled alongside of me and asked if I needed a beer. They handed me a can and were on their way, neither one of us having missed a stroke.

Yaht, now a town of a few hundred, once was a boom town with over 3500 people. Men came out here on the railroad to work in the lumber camps. A big hotel in town is a relic of bygone days. It was a good place to spend a Saturday evening. I met a couple of railroad workers and we had a few games of pool over some beers.

It was nearing the time when I should be crossing the Alberta boundary and leaving the mountains, an event I eagerly anticipated. A continuing problem was that I got up so late. It was eleven the next morning in Yaht before I had things packed up. And then 12:30 or 1:00 when I left town, after having eaten lunch in a restaurant. I also had to wait the passing of a short rainstorm.

But the day's travel went well. Once on the road to Cranbrook, the miles seemed to fly by. I stopped in little Moyie for a couple more hours to dodge some more rain. It seemed at last as if I were getting the feel of riding every day, and this habituation was pushing me on. Fifty miles at the beginning had seemed an onerous chore. Now fifty miles was just a matter of putting it in automatic pilot and sailing off. I knew one thing: this 50 to 80 miles-per-day output was going to have to be stepped up on the prairies. This resembled a lazy man's picnic on occasion. The majority of the days' travel began at 11:00 in the morning. That means ten or eleven hours' sleep a night. It might have been argued that the day's long exertion demanded eleven hours' regeneration. A more likely bet is that I was a little too lazy.

A mitigating factor was the blasted cold in the mornings. With one or two exceptions, each morning before sunrise it got excruciatingly cold. This cold reaches its apex — or maybe I should say nadir — just before the sun comes up and lasts an hour or two after sunrise. If I awoke during that time — and I most often did — I tried to make a self-contained heater of the whole mess by crawling deep into the sleeping bag, pulling my coat-cum-pillow after and folding the bag in on me so that things were nearly air-tight. Every warm exhalation was conserved to heat the system. And if it got very stuffy or insufferably cramped closed up in the sleeping bag, or if the lower digestive tract signaled the dénouement of the last meal — well then, I didn't have to come on the trip in the first place, did I?

There was no reason why that sleeping bag didn't do the job. It was not down-filled but that shouldn't have made any difference at temperatures of freezing or above. And it was well-protected by the tent from currents of cold air that could chill it. I've slept out in the bag on bare ground without a tent and everything was warm. It remains a mystery.

So many hours were lost in the morning because the cold was intimidating. It's hard to think of getting up, breaking down the tent and taking off when it is so cold. And then when the cold does abate, the memory of it is still there, and yours truly is giving the whole world the benefit of the doubt and remaining in the sack.

I saw one of the damnedest things I've ever run into the next day while riding about twenty or thirty miles south of Cranbrook. It happened near Elko.

There was frequent but not heavy traffic and it was about mid-day. I looked up at a passing pick-up and saw that it was on fire. You read right. And it wasn't the radiator that was overheated. The box of the pick-up was on fire; flames were two feet high. I had no idea what was going on as the truck drove on down the road. I ascribed it to some kids doing some pretty crazy joy-riding. How did I know what the local kids did for amusement?

Several miles farther on the road there was a long line of cars and it appeared at first that there had been a car accident. The line was backed up around a curve and as I rounded this curve, the cause of all this attention became apparent. The first car in the queue was about a block behind the old pick-up that had passed me a few minutes earlier. Only now the truck was in full conflagration, the twenty or so cars watching with trepidation, afraid of passing the truck — still on the road — less the gas tank explode in passing.

It was an eerie sight. The truck rested on the edge of the road on a level piece of ground. The flames had by this time spread from the box to engulf the cab. Shocked speculation on the presence or absence of people in the cab ran up and down the file of cars. All of a sudden, the truck began to move. It crawled slowly to the edge of the highway and the 100-foot drop below. It hardly looked as though the truck, after having remained stationary for some time, could have moved of its own accord. The truck edged slowly over the side of the road and then plummeted down the embankment. And at just the right time, about half way down, the gas tank exploded. It was just like in the movies.

I could have pushed the schedule that day and come close to the Continental Divide, maybe gone over it, but I needed a rest and felt like denying the bears a last chance.

All this last distance to the Continental Divide was uphill, of course, maybe fifty miles of it. But it was so gradual, nearly level, that riding was easy.

After having a good meal in Fernie, washing some

clothes and sleeping the sleep of the dead in a big old hotel bed, I started the next day with only 35 miles to the Continental Divide.

Whether or not it reflected the reality, I had come to think that it would be all downhill from the Continental Divide. I did not think that there could be many 8, 10 and 20 mile hills east of Alberta. I might have picked the 2500 mile point as a psychological watershed, so to speak. But it was the British Columbia - Alberta border where the mountains ended and so also did the long, arduous days of being slowed down by hills.

The Crowsnest Pass was the idée fixé in this case. And it was this goal, and the knowledge that it was thirty and then twenty miles distant, that mitigated the great strain of tackling the last of the Rockies.

These awesome mountains were going out like lambs though; the grades were most often quite gradual.

Given the beauty of the southern Canadian Rockies, it was disappointing to see the coal mining area at Natal, where the road makes the last great turn in the direction of the Crowsnest Pass. As is the case with coal mining areas nearly everywhere, this region had the look of a disaster area. Coal dust was everywhere and had long since blackened large parts of the region.

It was a short transit of a half hour or so and the only great inconvenience was dodging the massive coal trucks.

The mountains that guarded the Continental Divide were more spectacular and stately than had been the ones farther to the interior. And already I was feeling a nostalgia along with relief at leaving British Columbia. There would be none of this awesome scenery and no more of the crystal clear streams that ran from the lofty snowfields near the tops of the mountains.

But the Crowsnest Pass loomed ahead, both topographically and as a fixation of the mind. The road rose and the air turned cold.

Rounding a long curve that went up and to the right, I noticed in the distance a high cut where the road went along the mountain and then fell again. I had the feeling that this was the Crowsnest Pass, as it turned out to be. On reaching the top, which was 4280 feet, I celebrated in a very fitting fashion — with great gulps of British Columbia mountain stream water. The high point of the continent was a fait accompli.

Part Two

Chapter 10

It seemed that the ride down from the Crowsnest Pass would be little more than an anticlimax. As it developed, it was a very difficult stretch to negotiate. With the exception of small bits of satisfactory road, most of the highway was a two-lane affair without paved shoulders. In fact, virtually without any shoulders at all.

An interesting spot just into Alberta is the Frank slide site. In the early part of the century, a whole mountain side came crashing down on the village of Frank, killing 70 people. I was told that in the years since, this slide brought forth a new kind of prospecting. There were thousands of dollars in the Frank bank at the time of the slide. Many people since have tried to recover that money, thus far to no avail.

At this time in the trip, I had to take out a little time to attend a gathering of family and friends some distance away. I was fortunate to find a very helpful Chinese groceryman in Lundbreck who put the bike in a storage shed.

Once through visiting friends and relatives — too often these two groups are distinct — I headed back to Lundbreck to continue.

I had long wanted to see just how much distance I could cover in a day, and this day back in Lundbreck looked propitious. The chinook was blowing so this afforded a great boost travelling east. It was cool and cloudy so these were two more factors in favor of a good try.

I stocked up as much as I could on plums, milk and candy bars at the little grocery in order to reduce the need to stop during the day.

It was 1:30 p.m. when I started. I planned to ride as long as possible during the day, then to sleep and continue the following morning until 1:30 p.m. that afternoon, completing the twenty-four hour period.

The first part went exceedingly well. I had reached Lethbridge, a distance of 73 miles, in three and a half hours. 105 miles from Lundbreck on the road to Medicine Hat, the elapsed time was five and a half hours. I had stopped in Lethbridge for 15 minutes and two or three times for steep hills.

There was a long section of bad road between Lethbridge and Medicine Hat. It must have been nearly 50 miles in length. The road is a narrow, two-lane highway, patched quite a bit with no shoulders. To compound the problems, the edge of the highway was several inches above the ground so that when it was necessary to leave the road, I had to get off the bike to put it back on the pavement.

This horrendous section slowed the project somewhat but with the fast start of earlier in the day, the miles were beginning to add up.

The bad road ended 20 or so miles from Medicine Hat. It was nearly dark then so having a paved shoulder to ride on was a boon.

Still fifteen miles from Medicine Hat, the lights of the city came into view. They almost seemed for awhile as if they were receding. Approaching the city didn't seem to make the lights get any closer.

It turned quite cold after sunset. I got the gloves out and rolled down my long-sleeve shirt. Then for both warmth and visibility, I put the white undershirt over the long-sleeve shirt. A natty dresser I wasn't but it did the job.

When I was absolutely positive that the lights of Medicine Hat were going in the opposite direction as I was going toward them, I stopped and dug out something to eat, more for psychological relief than alimentary need.

It must have been a ludicrous sight. There was the bike on the paved shoulder and I beside it, sitting Indian-style and enjoying that little snack as if it were a feast.

After I had been sitting a few minutes, a car came from the opposite direction, passed me and then turned around. My first thought was that it was a motorist who was either curious or wanted to offer a ride. I also thought that, because it was Saturday night, it might be a drunk with who knows what on his mind.

The car came fast at me, going first off onto the shoulder and then into the ditch! I thought that I was really in for it. Who knew what that nut had in mind. But then, as soon as the car was abreast of me, it stopped and who should inquire about the state of things but an R.C.M.P. officer. Before even replying to his question, I asked him why he felt the need to approach me in the ditch. He didn't answer but went on to talk about something else, leaving me irritated at having been given a start by what at first had appeared to be a drunk or a lunatic. After a few more minutes of talking, he was off.

The wind had died down and it was cold. The prairie was soundless. It would have been an idyllic situation were it not for the cold and numbing fatigue that was beginning to overcome me after nearly 180 miles of riding.

The lights of Medicine Hat finally ceased their apparent receding and I pulled into town just after midnight. I pitched the tent just east of the city and slept a truly magnificent sleep. Heaven hath no reward like the surcease that comes from crawling into a warm sleeping bag after having ridden 180 miles.

I slept so long that night that rising late left little time to add to the mileage total of the day before. It must have been nearly eleven when I started out. By the time 1:30 p.m. came around, I had added 38 miles to the total, extending the miles covered that 24-hour period to 215. This was not only more miles than I had ever covered in a day but it was to be the longest distance covered during any day of the trip.

The rest of that day was easy riding, sort of a take-it-easy period after the previous day's all out effort.

I was now on the Trans-Canada Highway, planning to remain on it to Swift Current. The tourist traffic was very heavy on the highway. Everybody and his whole family was going on vacation. It's amazing to see the difference in traffic between the Trans-Canada and other highways. This is by far the most heavily-travelled and that's one of the main reasons my route rarely touched it. But the paved shoulders made the actual riding rather easy; traffic didn't interfere at all. They could move the whole population of Ontario to British Columbia along this road and you'd hardly give it notice.

For the first time, I met another fellow on bike going long distance. He was going west, travelling from Niagara Falls to British Columbia. The first thing I could think to ask him was an inane "Have you had any interesting experiences?" There is an immediate camaraderie that is established when two long-distance bikers meet. We looked at each other for a few seconds, almost with awe, and moved on.

For some reason, I felt like hell that day. I diagnosed it as general malaise compounded by searing heat, the cacophonous and continuous stream of traffic, an occasional but rueful hill, a seemingly unquenchable thirst and the haunting thought of four thousand miles yet to be travelled. My treatment for this was simple: moderate intake of food coupled with massive doses of liquid (not necessarily alcoholic) followed by a few hours of self-coddling. It's the only thing to get the juices moving again.

Accordingly, I limped (figuratively, mind you) into Swift Current. I bought, drank and relished one quart of root beer before even the merest thought of a burp entered my mind. I topped this off with a root beer float (notice a suggestion of monomania here?). Next came healthy amounts of cold water and the culinary bill of fare, fish and chips. Now, it must be said that ordinarily this oleaginous food wouldn't be good fare for an active stomach. But it wasn't the stomach that was speaking, it was the psyche.

Looking for anything as an excuse to avoid the road for a time, I went down to the public library to while away a couple of hours. For some reason — holiday I think — it was closed. I kicked the door. Biking psychosis was starting to set in. Anyone who assaults a public library is no friend of mine.

I recovered the will to move on after commiserating for a couple of hours, derelict-like, over glasses upon glasses of cold water.

It was mid-evening when I left Swift Current north for Saskatoon. I wanted to leave town slowly, peacefully, watch the sunset and take it easy.

As it was, another concern was foisted upon me; a smattering of foreboding cumulus clouds threatened to bring thunderstorms during the night. Although this chance didn't appear great, I wasn't in a mood to take any risks. A few days before, three U.S. professional golfers had survived a lightning bolt. I figured that if it could hit three guys making $100,000 a year, it could sure knock the hell out of me. And being hit by lightning could put a crimp in the itinerary, to say nothing of my future. I would probably have undergone a transformation of the sort that got Saul. On being hit by a bolt of lightning, I would get up, thank the Lord and rush to the nearest depot for a train ticket.

With the leisurely pace, I still made twenty miles that evening to the little village of Stewart Valley. This would at least, I felt, offer buildings and trees that would afford protection against lightning.

Off the Trans-Canada Highway for the first time in a long while, I saw clearly how there are really two Canadas. The one is a busy Canada adjusting itself readily to the fast pace of traffic and life along the main arteries of the country. It is a group of people which sees tourists all day long and is innured to them.

On the other hand, off the beaten path these little out-of-the-way villages exist almost untouched and they are quite something to see. Little colonies existing far out in the prairies all by themselves; they seem not to depend on larger cities.

There were no hotels or bars in Stewart Valley and only one store. It was hard to tell whether that was open at this hour, about 9 p.m. It was hard to tell even when I opened the door to the store and walked in.

The proprietor's family was seated at a counter at the opposite end of the store. They were eating their supper — late I take it — and watching television at the same time. It was hardly the sort of thing you'd see in the A & P.

There were things stocked in that store that looked as though they hadn't seen the light of day for a decade. It was ostensibly a grocery store but there were odds and ends of every sort. You could have found assorted hardware and maybe Christmas presents, depending on who was on your list that year. Most of the current items were things that looked like they moved regularly, like bread, milk and pop. The balance of the merchandise didn't look like it would move until a tornado hit the place.

Late the next morning, I chanced upon an interesting encounter. I had been running out of water when I saw a sign along the road offering fresh farm produce for sale. The sign pointed to a cluster of buildings about a mile from the road. I thought that it might be a good chance to stock up on milk.

The cluster of buildings turned out to be a Hutterite colony. Riding up to it, I was struck by the prosperous look of the buildings and machinery; all the buildings were either brand new or freshly painted. The crops, planted in great fields much larger than the usual, were already high. The whole impression of that of a highly efficient farming operation.

As I rode into the settlement itself, there was a group of men fitting a storage tank on some supports. The group was made up mostly of boys and young men and was led by a middle-aged man. They beckoned me to come over.

If Brigitte Bardot had walked into a prison, she wouldn't have attracted more attention than I did there. I asked about the milk but really didn't get an answer before being deluged with questions myself. They wanted to know the usual: where I came from, what the destination was, how many miles it was possible to cover in a day. But they were filled with other questions besides: Did I have a girlfriend? Did I know who they were? Had I seen many big cities? They had a thirst for information from the outside.

In the Hutterite culture, most contact with the outside is forbidden and much of the rest is frowned upon. Hence the absence of television, newspapers and most books. Hutterites have occasionally been seen, though, stationed in front of a television in a hotel lobby during their intermittent visits to town.

They did not sell milk along with poultry products but the elder of the group seemed willing to make an exception. But it was a hot day and he wanted to know how I was going to keep the milk. Did I have a refrigerator? I told him that I wasn't going to keep it. Half the quart of milk would be gone close to the instant of purchase and the other half wouldn't last out the hour.

The older man agreed and a younger boy was sent with me over to the milk house.

If ever there was a floor that you could have eaten from, that was it. The stainless steel milk tank shone. There was an ornate little notice, done in needlepoint, that was hung on the tank. It read "Please do not get your fingerprints on the milk tank."

The boy drew out a big ladle of milk with which I filled my water bottle. Then he drew out another big ladle full of milk and I drank that. This was rich, with the cream still mixed in.

Going back to where the others were, we passed a group of Hutterite women hurrying on their way somewhere. They still wore the long dresses and polka dot bonnets that they had always worn. No make-up adorned the faces. It seemed that nearly every one of them wore glasses. I wondered why. Only their optometrist knows for sure.

I continued on to Saskatoon where I had a very nice respite in the form of a stay of several days with a friend and his family. These long rests, nice as they are, make getting back on the bicycle more difficult. The muscles get flabby too quickly and once back riding it takes a few days for them to get back in shape.

The first technical problem occurred about this time. The neck of the water bottle tore. It was thus impossible to drink from the bottle without having water run out onto the chin. I replaced this with a plastic canteen nearly twice as large as the water bottle had been, looking forward to the increased carrying capacity of the canteen.

I left Saskatoon for the north toward what was to be the northernmost part of the trip, Prince Albert National Park.

These were still the prairies but the country slowly began to change. There were more and more trees, mostly deciduous but with the occasional conifer mixed in. The country also became more hilly.

At Rosthern, I turned east on a black-top road towards Batoche, along the banks of the South Saskatchewan River. After crossing the bridge on the river, it was necessary to go along a gravel road that followed the river for a distance of 23 miles, to a village called St. Louis. Five miles along this road was the Batoche battle site.

It's a beautiful place, actually. The river meanders below bluffs that are a couple of hundred feet high. In the old cemetery near the church there are graves of many of those who fought with Riel, including Gabriel Dumont, the great buffalo hunter. The many other graves are those of the French who were buried there from before the rebellion to the present day. Included in these latter is a recent one with a sad, and rather modern, note. It is the grave of Louise Poulin "victime de la folie d'un malheureux à Londres" who died in the summer of 1973 when she was 22 years old.

There are still many Métis living around the Batoche site, several of them descendants of those who fought with Riel.

The gravel road to St. Louis was not a gift, as the French say. I never knew which sharp rock would be the one to break the string of good luck enjoyed by my tires for 1300 miles. But it was peaceful riding in the early evening hours without any cars.

While riding along the road, I saw something ahead that was very long and narrow, winding slowly across the road. It looked like a boa constrictor!

With a little intelligent reflection and upon moving closer, I saw that it was a mother duck and a long line of faithful ducklings, following her turn for turn and waddle for waddle across the road. Those fuzzy little creatures wouldn't have had the foggiest notion of where they were going without their mother. I slowed down to let the expedition pass.

This whole part of the trip was made more pleasant by the presence along the road of a very fragrant blue plant. I took it to be a weed and sketched it in the hopes I could find out what it was later. Its aroma was an ever-present perfume that stayed with me, enhancing the many visual pleasures with an olfactory delight.

Someone along the road had told me that St. Louis was a French village. As I at long last approached it, the first thing that stood out was a large church with its silver spire. These silver spires mark nearly every village in Québec. And unlike some nondescript little Protestant church, these churches and their spires announce their presence for miles across the countryside.

I headed for the first hotel and its beverage room. A conversation wasn't long in starting. There were three people at the next table, two women and a man. One of the women had been talking to the other in French so I began in French also. As it turned out, the man didn't speak French. The strange thing was that the parents of all the three were French; the young man had forgotten the language in which he had grown up. The attrition rate of one third at that table may have been a representative figure of what occurs with French populations outside the province of Québec. And then people wonder why the Québécois seem so obstreperous. It just may be because they are the only ethnic group to have enough pride in their language and culture to fight assimilation. Italians, Ukrainians, Poles and especially the Indians and the Eskimos — all are losing their special identities in front of the ethnocentric Anglo-Saxon tidal wave. And the Québécois are the only ones with the courage to fight it. They're the only ones to believe it could be as natural and practical to speak French as it is to speak English.

French is fast losing ground in the French villages of Saskatchewan. These three people told me that their schools offered an hour of French class each day. Which is about the same as Calgary or San Antonio, Texas. In any case, it is truly nothing next to the schools where all the classes all day long are given in French; here the language is learned through instruction and through osmosis.

Anyway, our conversation was enlightening if not too long. I had to leave town before sunset to set up camp.

The woods now covered the land again. The place I picked for the tent was wooded and bushy, with all the mosquitoes that usually go with such terrain.

Mosquitoes, for those readers who have never been in the bush, are a scourge. They do not leave you with a moment's peace. They are impossible, exasperating, irritating and they engender more pique and bald anger than all the rest of mankind's banes. Why can't some Canadians do with the mosquito what George Washington Carver did with the peanut? They should elect a mosquito prime minister of Canada. They come in contact with more of the people than Trudeau ever will. They could have put a mosquito on the Canadian flag instead of the maple leaf. There certainly must be more mosquitoes in this country than maple leaves. From the Rockies to the forests around Prince Albert, I didn't see a single maple leaf. The mosquito, unfortunately, was well-represented. Delegations numbering well into the hundreds were sent to each of the places I pitched my tent.

And here it was the same. The mosquito netting works well, luckily. I pile sleeping bag, jacket and whatever else has to go into the tent that night just in front of the tent. Then in a flash, I unzip the screen in the tent, throw in the gear and jump in after it, turning around quickly to close the screen. There's a little open area at the bottom of the tent where the three zippers come together. I fill this by stuffing a small rag there and pulling the zipper down to it. It keeps the inside of the tent pretty well impervious to mosquitoes. Once inside the tent, I slap the few remaining mosquitoes that have made it inside with me.

And yet there are forty or fifty mosquitoes still buzzing at the screen trying to get in. If a person wanted to commit hari-kari with mosquitoes, all he'd have to do is unzip the screen and lie back.

Alas, the problems aren't as simple as this. Not only is this country populated by Canadians, white-tailed deer and mosquitoes, but there are other perfidious, ubiquitous creatures abroad in the land. They're called no-see-ums. I am able to report that you can see 'um. But apart from that, they have a lot that is to their strategic advantage. They pass rather easily through the aforementioned screen. They begin attacking and have a good (for them) mouthful of your leg before you're able to tell they are there. These creatures, along with their spiritual brothers the mosquitoes and the black flies, are all part of any close contact with the Canadian bush.

Chapter 11

I awoke the next morning rather early, at six o'clock. It must have been fairly early because I arrived in Prince Albert before eight.

Prince Albert is the city of John Diefenbaker. He is duly commemorated by a bridge there, along with who knows what else. But I crossed the bridge so that was the only thing I saw.

I was hoping to get all the way to Prince Albert National Park that day. I had it in mind to visit the homeground of one of the most intriguing characters Canada has ever produced, a man who is nearly legendary now. His name is Grey Owl.

Grey Owl wasn't really an Indian. But they didn't find that out until later and it doesn't really matter. This man did as much for conservation as any man of his time. It is a man's way of thinking and acting that counts. The spirit determines the man. And of Grey Owl it can truly be said that he was Indian and a man of the wilderness. He always spelled wilderness with a capital "W" as if it were a country. To him it was, as much a separate domain as the United States or Canada.

His day spanned the first third of this century, when men still travelled through the wilderness by canoe and when there were many Indians to be found who were still living in the Indian way. They called him Grey Owl because of his habit of travelling by night.

All he knew of the woods he learned from the Indians and the white trappers. He himself lived as a trapper in the early years, earning his livelihood from this, first around Biscotasing in Ontario and later in the Abitibi region in Québec.

Then he met and fell in love with an Indian girl, Anahareo, and because of her aversion to the pain inflicted upon trapped animals, Grey Owl soon turned from trapping. It was about this time also that he turned to writing, first with some articles in outdoor magazines and then, at the urging of his magazine editors, he began writing books. And the books began to sell tremendously. His power to evoke the spirit of the wilderness hasn't been matched. He combined the conservationist's love of the land, the sensitive human being's regard for the Indian and his vanishing way of life with the art of the writer. And what a skill! Much of his prose ranks with the best in Canadian literature and far surpasses a lot of that which passes as literature. Although literature that speaks of the wilderness is often déclassé, his art rings true, not only as a paean to the wilderness and a plea for its preservation, but also as a literary achievement in its own right.

I'd like to go on writing of Grey Owl. But my own ability to evoke the man and his land is quite inferior to his power to make the spirit of the wilderness live on the printed page and in the hearts of people in distant lands.

Grey Owl is at his best in *Pilgrims of the Wild*, where he tells the true story of his falling in love with Anahareo and how they came to protect the beaver.

There are several films extant of Grey Owl, including some he made himself. The best ones show him at Lake Ajawaan in Prince Albert National Park with Rawhide and Jelly Roll, the two beavers he made famous, and who made him famous.

In the summer, Grey Owl and Anahareo shared a duplex, you might call it, with Jelly Roll and Rawhide.

Grey Owl had a log cabin down by the lake. The beaver lodge had two entrances, one inside the cabin and one outside. The outside entrance was underwater. Jelly Roll and Rawhide used this when they wanted to enter from the lake. When they were bringing building materials or had another excuse for entering by land, they went through Grey Owl's front door. Grey Owl would often be writing and answer a tap on the door to find one of the beaver standing on its hind legs and balancing a load of twigs and mud between its paws. Then the beaver would either walk across the floor with the load or, if it were heavy, drop the building materials and push them across the floor to the entrance of the lodge. Grey Owl would then witness their building procedures.

Grey Owl was the godfather, after a fashion, to the pups of Jelly Roll and Rawhide. He could see Jelly Roll was pregnant and one day she entered the lodge and a few days later Grey Owl could hear the squealing of the offspring. Jelly Roll didn't bring them out right away but kept them in the lodge for a few weeks. When she did bring it out, she brought the pup to Grey Owl and handed it to him for his approval. Grey Owl helped the little pup along by supplementing its diet with milk from a bottle.

Grey Owl lived in a cabin at the north end of Ajawaan Lake which is near Kingsmere Lake in Prince Albert National Park.

After a long day of riding north from Prince Albert into a strong headwind, I finally came to the park. The park charges a fee to motorized traffic, including motorcycles. But bicycles enter free. A nice gesture.

I found that there was a canoe available at the Narrows along the south shore of Waskesiu Lake and so began going in that direction toward nightfall.

I made camp in a place on a bank next to the lake that I could see was covered with poison ivy. There didn't seem to be any ill effects, however.

At the Narrows, they warned me how rough it could

get on Kingsmere Lake, the big lake just above Waskesiu Lake. This latter was already a bit choppy and with a northwest wind, it was no telling what Kingsmere would be like.

I set off from the Narrows with tent, sleeping bag, food and odds and ends packed in the canoe.

Waskesiu Lake was pleasant although a little choppy. It took only two hours to go the seven or eight miles to Kingsmere River at the west end of the lake. Except for the mosquitoes, it was fairly easy to negotiate the river and the 200-yard portage that went along with it.

But then the troubles started. There was a strong wind blowing directly from the north shore to the outlet at Kingsmere River on the south. The waves were bad. There wasn't much choice of alternatives. I would hit big waves but hit them straight on if I went directly across the lake. To take either the eastern or western shore of the lake would mean waves that were smaller. But then they would be abeam and more dangerous yet.

I opted for the direct route across. No sooner had I started than I was nearly swamped by a wave that broke over the bow. The best I could do was move the sleeping bag, tent and food a little out of the water; there was no hope of giving any attention to bailing the water out; while the waves were high I had to do everything I could to keep the canoe afloat.

In fact, the main task all the way across was not so much making forward progress as avoiding capsizing. For this reason it took nearly six hours to cross the nine miles to the north end of the lake. It was constantly necessary to give a forward stroke with the paddle and then to switch quickly to a steadying stroke so the waves wouldn't turn the canoe around. That was certainly the closest that the trip had come so far to disaster.

When I finally reached the other shore my arms and shoulders were nearly numb from the six hours of constant work and tension. I found a little outcropping on the lake where the mosquitoes were blown away by the wind and there I lay for a half hour, gasping and exhausted.

I portaged a short distance and was then on the shores of Ajawaan Lake, smaller than Kingsmere fortunately.

Grey Owl's cabin was on the northwest side of the lake. It was a small lake, quite serene at this time, late evening. I pulled ashore a few feet from his cabin.

It was a beautiful spot. The cabin where the beaver had also lived was still by the side of the lake. Its log structure was sagging a little but not bad considering it is forty years since Grey Owl lived there. The inside of the cabin is still in fairly good shape; his bed is still there. It is easy to imagine him there, living his Walden-like existence and content with his simple life. Indeed, he has often been compared to Thoreau because of his espousal of the simple life out of doors and to St. Francis of Assisi for his intimate relationship with the animals.

The birds, beaver and many other creatures came to eat out of his hand. He even compiled a beaver dictionary cataloguing the sounds he used to communicate with the beaver.

Above the lake cabin on a rise is the cabin in which he passed his winters. His grave is here too. His monument is the only one he ever wanted or needed . . . the Wilderness.

I tented near the lower cabin and had a supper of herring and peanuts.

The night there was outstanding. The mosquitoes for some reason had occupied themselves elsewhere. The wind had died and an hour after nightfall everything was unimaginably still and quiet. Then from the north began a stream of aurora borealis across the sky. From its origin in the north, the lights — two beams in the form of undulating curtains — stretched through the zenith and toward the southern pole. They were a wonder to watch, these mysterious beacons arcing back and forth over the silent black forest. The sleep I slept that night was as fine as I had ever had.

Next morning brought something I had been waiting for, albeit with a little trepidation, since long ago and far away in British Columbia — a visit by a bear.

The tent, as already mentioned, was near the lake. I was going up from the tent to where I had eaten, just a few yards up from the shore. I saw a black form moving through the woods toward the area where the food was. It was neither, I found out quickly to my chagrin, a deer nor a moose. It was a black bear and he had me spotted at about the same time I realized what I was facing. I had been anticipating the first contact with a bear for a long time. What was there to do? I would have thought, especially during all those nights of imaginings in the tent, that the most likely move would be to throw the bear the food at hand, climb a tree and hope for the best.

Strangely, now that the situation was at hand (but not yet in hand), the bear and I both remained unruffled, which at least is more than I expected of myself under the circumstances.

I watched the animal with great curiosity even as he watched me. There was a little breeze from the lake so the bear got my scent immediately. After the many days I had spent without a bath recently, no wonder he didn't come any closer. But he did want to have a look at the food. So he stayed around for nearly an hour. While I wrote in my notebook, he continued to make semi-circles around me from water's edge to water's edge. And every few feet of his semi-circle, he would stop, look at me, sniff and continue circling. He was either waiting for me to leave so he could get at the food, or he wanted me to take a bath. I'm not sure which. He finally left and I went on writing, surprised and happy that our encounter had been so tranquil.

It was not an hour later when I again heard some movement in the bush nearby. I half expected it to be the black bear back to see if I had left. This was a bear all right, but not the same one. This visitor was a larger cinnamon-coloured behemoth. When it rains, it pours!

I don't know what I had done to deserve all these visits. Maybe not taking a dip in the lake had had something to do with it.

This bear was also interested in the food but he seemed a bit more determined in his quest of it. He didn't circle the tent but rather remained near the lake, sitting for a while in some tall grass, scratching his nose and then getting up and taking a walk closer to me to see what the story was. He gave the impression of a certain degree of impatience, unlike the other bear who was willing to bide his time. If I had been wavering about when to break camp, this helped me to decide. And so with one eye on the bear and the other on the tent, I pulled out the stakes, humming nonchalantly as I did so, hoping that the bear would think that I had planned on moving along at this time anyway. He looked on as I put the gear into the canoe and pushed away with consummate insouciance.

Lake Ajawaan was flat as glass; the wind of the previous day was gone. Kingsmere was as pacific this day as it had been violent the day before. The crossing was idyllic; there wasn't a cloud in the sky nor a ripple on the water.

These lakes in this area, the larger ones at least, Kingsmere and Waskesiu, are so pure that you can drink out of them. And the water is nothing less than delicious. I had taken some water from the spigot at the park headquarters in Waskesiu and had marvelled at its good taste. After hundreds of miles of hot days, I fancied myself as something of a connoisseur of fine water. This water, I was told, had come from the lake.

Out on the lake in the canoe, the canteen could be dipped in anywhere for a drink. The water was cool and very soft. Some of the water in the southern prairies would have made your hair stand on end. Its only true use was filling the car radiator. But here the water was beautiful.

I returned the canoe at the Narrows after a surprisingly easy voyage back. It was amazing how different the two trips had been.

It now remained for me to retrace my path for more than fifty miles, the first time that I had done this.

The trip back was without the headwind I had had to contend with earlier so the going was easy. It was hot, though, and in the space of several hours, I drank four glasses of beer, four bottles of pop, two malted milks, a quart of whole milk and a canteen full of water.

The whole area north of Prince Albert is a tourist region. For the most part, the vistors come from other areas of Saskatchewan and a great number come from Alberta. The most interesting ones come, invariably, from the United States. Among this group are a certain number for whom this is the first visit to Canada. And the normal thing then is to expect that they ask the sort of questions that exasperate Canadians. Canada has never suffered from over-exposure and often feels that the United States regards this country either as an inferior or leaves it out of the picture altogether, not taking the time to learn anything about Canada. Questions of this nature tend to reinforce these feelings:

"How come you don't take American stamps up here?"
"Montréal, isn't that the capital of Canada?"
"Does everyone speak French in Canada?"
"Is there snow all year there?"
"Canada, is that a country?"

And I don't even dare to quote the more inane statements. Canadians suffer it well, however, and only occasionally give in to the strain. Canadians, Australian aborigines and Siberian tigers all have one thing in common — they're not Americans. And they share everything that, for better or worse, this entails. There are more and more Canadians who are happy at the distinction.

Chapter 12

I had purposely avoided campgrounds until now. For one thing, it isn't easy to stop at the end of the day precisely where a campground is located. Then there is a certain noise factor that goes along with staying in a camping area. Part of the idea of travelling in the first place is being alone, seeing new things — not other tourists. Sometimes — but just sometimes — there are fewer mosquitoes in campgrounds. Frequently the reverse seems to be true.

Some of these campers come equipped with everything but the kitchen sink. Take it back; they even have that. They're able to do for themselves anything that Holiday Inn could have done for them. Some of the camper assemblies boggle the mind. Motorbikes, boats, bicycles and lawn chairs strapped in every available place all over the camper. Some of the self-driven behemoths are so costly that the interest alone on the purchase of the thing should be sufficient to rent a reasonable camper for the few weeks that most people have available for vacation. I remember once riding to school with a political science professor of mine. We were riding in his souped-up, all-equipped, five-miles-per-gallon house on wheels. It reminded me of what Thoreau had written: "And when the farmer has got his house, he may not be the richer but the poorer for it, and it may be the house that has got him." And I thought, buddy, have you been had.

In Melfort, southeast of Prince Albert, there was a sign indicating a local campground. The land was fairly free of forests again and most of it was taken up with farming. So I took the plunge and went to the campground, sure (I thought) of a good place to stay.

It was of the kind that was well-foliated, with high brush at least. Each camping area was separated from the others by this brush. No sooner had I stopped, before even leaving the bike, than the mosquitoes gave notice that sponsorship by the Saskatchewan government in no way abrogated their territorial rights to the area. I was getting amazingly fast at setting up that tent faced with the hordes of mosquitoes. I quickly got off the bike, loosened the cord on back that bound the sleeping bag and tent to the back of the bike and threw that pack to the ground. I had already rolled down the sleeves on my shirt and then I quickly unrolled the sleeping bag to fish out the long pants I had stored inside. I took off the shorts and put on the pants, also in great haste. With this fair amount of protection, the only bad areas to protect were the face and hands. That is, unless the mosquitoes are particularly plentiful. In that case, the extra measure of pulling the socks up over the bottoms of the pants helps to keep the mosquitoes from going up the pant legs. I had just read an article by a fellow who said that in a wilderness situation it is better to have no cover in order to better see the stars, or a rain fly in order to get the most contact with the outdoors. He failed to say whether he thought the mosquitoes would lie back and look at the stars with him. What a dreamer!

Anyway, back to the tent. Once clothed against the mosquitoes, I dumped the tent, stakes and poles from the plastic bag which contained them. Moving only a little more slowly than the mosquitoes, I unrolled the tent, unfolded it and took four stakes around to the corners, one to each as logic would have it, and stuck them into the ground. Occasionally, if the ground is hard, this requires the aid of a piece of wood as a driver. Then — and this is the tricky part with 400 mosquitoes buzzing nearby who all want some of your blood — I fit the tent pole sections together, taking time to see that the ends are joined in the right places so that the mosquitoes don't have a few more minutes to exact their tribute. Then the poles go through an eyelet on each end of the tent and stakes go in at each end to secure the cords that brace the poles. Two stakes to pull out the cords that pull out the sides of the tent complete the operation.

Any deviation from the smooth completion of this procedure gives rise to great perturbation and not a little profanity. Hell hath no fury like that of 400 mosquitoes only a skin's thickness away from twelve pints of warm blood.

Thus completes the rite of pitching, although rite connotes a certain deliberation and doesn't really reflect the great haste that goes into it.

If it got especially hot, I tied open the rear window and the front flap. This made it cooler with the circulating air and helped to avoid condensation in the morning. If it had been cold, a closed tent helped to retain body heat.

Now came the entrance procedure.

I took all the necessary things for the night from the bags on the bike. If I'm thirsty, I grab a fast drink from the canteen.

Then all these items — sleeping bag, jacket-cum-pillow, perhaps a book — and the other odds and ends were placed next to the door of the tent.

In a motion which would compare in speed to that of a man who has just sat on a hot stove, I unzipped the door of the tent, threw in the things, jumped in after and rezipped the door of the tent. And the blessed little tent was just about bug-proof then. A little rag filling up the juncture where the zippers meet virtually ensures a mosquito-free tent. It remains, however, to kill those few who have entered the tent along with me.

The mosquitoes didn't do it all that night though. It was a Saturday night and there was a series of joy-riders speeding through the grounds. This orgy of adolescence was culminated by a beer party, a loud one, that lasted until sunrise. So it was a poor introduction to campgrounds.

Nevertheless, the following night I found myself staying in another one. After riding over a road that was becoming worse and worse, I came to the Greenwater State Park. I don't know where they got all the people to fill that park, but full it was. What a good chance to have a swim and read leisurely while drying off on the beach. There are a lot of problems with swimming in lakes out here. Either there aren't any, or the ones that exist are too marshy or have some other drawback. There are none to compare with the likes of Kingsmere Lake in the north.

Bears are seen in this park quite frequently. But except for this area, bears don't too often venture south of the forests, which are perhaps a hundred miles to the north. Wolves have occasionally been spotted in the region.

Wolves, I believe, have a very bad reputation, and unjustifiably so. They're often blamed for depredations far beyond the needs of their own consumption. And they are often accused as a cover-up for some of the damage man has done. They are occasionally accused of endangering whole species with which they have co-existed for millenia. They're too often easy scapegoats.

There is a predator out here far more rapacious than the wolf, more rapacious even than the most ardent of the wolf's detractors would have us believe he is. In fact, this predator is found in lesser or greater numbers in every province of Canada, although in some it is beneficiently more scarce.

It's a strange animal, often killing far more than it needs for its own food, leaving game behind in many cases. The wolf has been accused of endangering several species; there is definite proof that this predator has in fact completely annihilated many species.

This animal exhibits behaviour that is all out of place with that of other members of the animal kingdom. It occasionally kills its own kind when hunting other animals.

Not only does this animal have a higher capacity for the decimation of other animals, it also has an astonishing propensity for self-destruction. Some animals are known to commit suicide; this one has a particularly high rate.

Like many animals, the more it is forced to live close to its own kind, the more there is a tendency to anxiety that leads it to want to kill others of its own species. Indeed, there is evidence of this animal's actually having killed more than 50,000,000 of its own kind in the last four decades.

In a particularly demented practice, this animal has been known to put to death, in a somewhat ritualistic manner, a member of the group who has committed some grave transgression. And the execution, as it were, is carried out deliberately and with the assent and in the presence of several other members of the group.

This predator, of course, is man.

There isn't much to report about eastern Saskatchewan, except that it's there. Often it is very worthwhile to travel through an area even though there is nothing, seemingly, of interest to see. Even though a region may only be dotted with small towns connected by narrow asphalt and gravel roads and be devoid of lakes and other things of natural interest, travelling through the section gives you a sense of space, helps put all the other areas in perspective. And space is what Canada is all about.

This was an area populated more and more by Ukrainians. Villages with large Ukrainian populations have the inevitable Ukrainian Catholic Church somewhere within their limits. These churches, with their distinctive Byzantine steeples, announce the religion and nationality as effectively as do the lofty silver steeples of the French churches.

Bicycling may be a little slow and at times arduous but it is certainly one of the best ways to know the land and its people. If you want to know Nature, there is no finer way to travel than by canoe, for this sort of living demands an intimacy with the outdoors that few means of transportation can match. If you want to know stewardesses, then fly. But if you want to know as much of the land and the people who built it as possible, then you must travel the highways and the country roads — especially the country roads. And you must go as slowly as you can. The people are remarkably friendly; their life is slow-paced, their goals modest and family-oriented.

I cooked out on this trip and I bought fruit and nuts to eat on the road but the special treats were always the stops in the little out of the way restaurants and cafes. In many of these places, you might just be the only customer all week whom the proprietor did not know personally. And then you're a special guest, receiving service as you would have had you been a guest in his home. In fact, that nearly is the case sometimes because the restaurant's kitchen is often the family kitchen. You know the food is homemade.

I remember just such a restaurant. There was no other customer so the lady had time to offer a lot of attention. It was quiet in the area which was not truly a village. The road didn't even have the proverbial widening. There were no more than a handful of houses; the one directly across the road from the restaurant window was a neat bungalow of not too old vintage. It was surrounded by a white picket fence whose tops were painted in blue to go with the trim on the house. The house, although modern, had an old vestigial outhouse in the rear, if outhouses can be vestigial. I once knew a farmer who continued to use the old outhouse on his farm for many years after the toilet was installed indoors. Such sentimentality is rare indeed.

It was noon and one of the reasons for stopping was a threatening thunderstorm. It was the path of the storm that was in question. It appeared that it would cross the road ahead, but if it didn't, it could have caused problems. I didn't know if the tires on the bike would be good insulation from the ground. A wet tire lessens the chance of insulation and then of course lightning will travel through any substance if the charge is strong enough and the distance sufficiently short. I once was travelling along a wet road at night when lightning struck the road ahead. The charge went along the road, through the wet tires of the bike and gave a mighty jolt to him who was riding the thing.

So it was raining like mad with lightning and thunder completing the orchestration. They were pleasant moments inside when it was stormy outside. The rest was welcome and it was a good chance to get in a little reading.

One typical day in the life of this trip went something like this:

I have spent the night in a small picnic area near a lake a couple miles east of Preeceville, Saskatchewan. It wasn't easy doing that either because I had come late when it was dark and could only see the sign indicating the area by the light of cars passing from time to time. Feeling the way in the dark, I set up the tent. Because the air had been still and the area so close to the lake, the mosquitoes were especially bad.

Having camped next to a well was convenient; the next day I rose and was able to brush my teeth right away, something rather unusual, and fill the canteen. This water is still of the prairie variety and no real treat to drink but it does the job. The nostalgia for the mountain water in British Columbia and the water at Kingsmere Lake is creeping back again.

The wind is good this day. That means it's a tail wind. The ride to Swan River, Manitoba should go well. My high gear on the bicycle is a mite temperamental due to a loose gear cable. When I want to ride in high now, being a little too lazy to spend ten minutes alleviating the problem, I have to kick the chain to get it in gear. Now before getting on, I manoeuvre it into high gear while walking alongside. Then I get on the bike, throwing the leg over the front wheel and handlebars because the tent and gear are packed high on the back.

It feels good to harness this westwind. The crank turns slowly — this is the highest gear — and slowly this whole agglomeration gets a little motion in it. Soon speed picks up and it becomes fast enough for the high gear to handle.

It is about nine-thirty now. The sun is in my face but the passing breeze keeps things cool.

The bike is moving well. The muscles feel good — not strained — and it feels good to keep up a fast speed. I'm coasting at about 25 miles-per-hour.

In quick succession, I pass Sturgis, Stenen and Hyas, all about seven or eight miles apart.

I often leave in the morning before eating, feeling that a few miles in the morning without anything in the stomach is good for the system. If it is possible to get in twenty or even forty miles without eating, I do it. Today, I have a notion to stop at Norquay, partly because of its name, partly because it represents an already creditable twenty-seven miles travelled. Once at Norquay however, enthusiasm for the road and the day takes over and I continue straight through, ready to ride on while things are going so well.

A sweat is starting to develop. When you work you sweat. When you sweat you feel good. And when you feel good like this, you're really alive.

There are sloughs by the road, marshy affairs that breed mosquitoes and a plethora of waterfowl. Ducks swim in the sloughs by the hundreds, with the ducklings that are now starting to gain size. Silent as a bike is, these ducks are sometimes frightened as it passes. Then the mother takes off like a shot, sometimes leaving the young ones behind. Occasionally, a single duck will be swimming near the road when I pass on the bike. Then the duck sticks his neck up, looks around and, faster than I could blink, he dives under water.

Swallows nest in these rushes as well. They're nesting at this time of year. As the bike passes, they're alerted so the adults take to the wing and go after the interloper (me). And the whole flock takes turns diving at me, occasionally dropping so close that they nearly hit my head. I keep on moving — fast — and wave my arms to ward them off. About this time a car passes from the opposite direction and the occupants think that I am wildly and enthusiastically waving to them and so they wave back just as enthusiastically.

The sun is shining down directly from in front. An hour or two later and it will be coming from the side. That will make riding easier. That is another reason why riding west to east is a good idea. It is much less tiring to have the sun shining in the face for a few hours in the morning than having the light coming directly in the eyes in the evening after a day's hard riding.

I leave the undershirt on today. It is getting annoying to have to guard against sunburn so frequently. Leave the shirt off for a couple of hours and you'd think things would be all right but then a sunburn develops later, and a sunburn can ruin a night's sleep.

The day is hot but the air is fresh and scented. Newly-mown hay on both sides of the road is a pleasure to smell. Once in a while, large patches of wild roses announce their presence with a beautiful fragrance that wafts over the road.

I drink water from the canteen while still on the bike. It is such a joy today to ride that I have no desire to get off the bike. The water has been laced with an orange drink and tastes good. This orange drink satisfies the thirst when the water is warm. I've begun using this stuff on the prairies from time to time because of the dire necessity of making this water potable. It kills the taste of the water.

The bike moves along, the green fields and farm houses hidden in groves of trees moving by slowly. The towns can be seen several miles off. Each has its two or three grain elevators that, in an abstract sense and from a distance, look like huge dolls standing as sentinels out in the prairie.

Each of these little communities is a little enclave with a gas station or two, a church that fits the ethnic and religious make-up of the village, and a general store. If the place is a little larger, there is a hotel, its beverage room the centre of the town social life, at least for the wets.

After more than fifty miles on the bike, and before I stop for something to eat, another frontier creeps up, this one the Manitoba - Saskatchewan border. Suddenly and strangely, British Columbia seems a very long distance away. Is it possible that I have spanned all those miles? A feeling for the breadth of the country is present as it hadn't been in Saskatchewan only a few days before. The east isn't far away.

I stop in Benito finally about mid-afternoon. Funny the names given to some of these places. In a little restaurant in town I order a hamburger, buy a newspaper and settle down to read. The reading of newspapers is another pleasure that is magnified after a strenuous few hours' riding. The thirst receives attention too. The waitress brings two glasses of water, each with ice. After the water is gone, I have two bottles of cola poured over the ice. The drink is quite cold and couldn't be more effective in satisfying the thirst.

I move out of Benito after about an hour on a 20-mile leg to Swan River. There's a train track paralleling the road and a train passes not much faster than I'm going. The engineer of the train opens the whistle in salutation.

The road goes north, east, north, east and finally makes a last turn north to reach Swan River. The town is small and fairly still at this time of the evening, just after supper time.

There's a hotel at the side of the road and this appeals as a good opportunity for something cold. I enter assuming that I will travel a few miles yet this evening before stopping.

But as luck would have it, good luck certainly, there's a roisterous group in the tavern and after having a few glasses and something to eat, I fall in with them. There are a couple of girls and a few men. The bicycle trip doesn't remain the centre of conversation long, fortunately, and before long everyone in the group has given a rundown on his or her work.

One thing leads to the next; beer flows and the stories get longer and longer and the next thing I know the whole evening has gone by and it is nearly midnight. A farewell to the friends and I'm out on the road again for a few miles to find a camping place.

So that's a fairly typical day in the life of this trip. The riding was a little smoother and the evening a little more jovial than most maybe but you get the idea.

Chapter 13

I ran into an interesting little fellow in Dauphin while visiting the park there. The swimming pool was just closing as I came up to it. Hot and weary, I must have had a disappointed look.

This young man, who undoubtedly hadn't yet seen six years, was standing near the entrance to the pool, having just come out it seemed, and had more knowledge of the situation than I. So I asked him if the pool was closed.

"I think so," he said, somewhat regretfully in sympathy with my plight.

"No one is allowed in any more?"

"That's right," he told me.

"Do you suppose a person might . . . uh . . . sneak in?" I asked him, hoping he would treat this idea with the proper discretion.

"I suppose so," said he. "That must be how burglars take a bath."

". . . !"

It was some time later than this that I was to begin a modest little experiment that had a rather strange result.

I had long been lamenting the fact that I felt forced to sleep in the tent every night, sorry that I wasn't seeing the trees and stars above when drifting off to sleep.

So the idea was to find a place free of mosquitoes. To begin with, it was hard to believe that such a place existed in Canada, unless it be in downtown Toronto perhaps. But finally I got lucky. Going along the road in the evening, I spied a mound with a handful of nice leafy popple trees. And, what was better, there was virtually no ground foliage under the trees. In other words, it wasn't a place conducive to mosquitoes. The little breeze that was blowing also helped.

Unfortunately, the timing could have been off a little; it threatened to rain.

Nevertheless, I stopped, unpacked the gear and made a little supper. I wanted to wait a little before deciding whether to put the tent up.

Supper finished, I took a look at the sky and thought what the hell. It was one of those low overcast skies that looks like it might bring rain and then again might not. But I was going ahead with it.

I crawled into the sleeping bag just as the last of the twilight was fading into darkness.

Just as I got settled, a few drops of rain fell. Nothing to worry about but definitely an unfavourable portent for later. There is nothing worse than trying to get your wits together to attempt to deal with a situation when it's just after midnight and you're soaking wet. This worry boded ill for my sleep.

I curled up in the sleeping bag, as much against the coolness of the evening as against the odd mosquito passing by.

The thought that occupied my mind was whether it was going to rain and if it did, what was I going to do about it? I sorted through a few alternatives. I could stay in the cold, soaking sleeping bag all night. I've been in worse situations. (I must have, haven't I?) Scratch that. Too masochistic. I could run to the nearest shelter (twelve miles away?!). No hope for that idea. Or I could jump out of the sleeping bag and quickly put up the tent. A lousy idea, but then the other two didn't even qualify that far. And the tent is water-proof, at least in a metaphysical sense.

So that was it then. At the first sign of serious rain, I would spare myself the more through a hasty mounting of the tent. Excellent.

Now the only problem that remained was to get to sleep. This thought of rain bothered me continuously and wouldn't let me sleep. There had been no more rain but it looked rainy. That's all. It just looked rainy.

Finally, almost miraculously, I fell off to sleep.

But the sleep was not to remain undisturbed. Several hours later, at the first hint of morninglight, I again regained semi-consciousness. In this state and still bunched up in the sleeping bag, I immediately recalled my earlier fear of rain. But as nearly as I could tell, it had not rained during the night. At least it did not seem that the sleeping bag was wet. I was, however, much too lazy to stick my neck out and see. I had been tired from the day before and every extra few minutes of sleep was needed. Oh well, I thought, if it rains now, then at least I will have gotten some sleep and, if not, quite to the good.

Then I heard it. Drop, drop, drop. A few sprinkles of rain. Still groggy and not willing to open an eye, I remained in the sleeping bag, telling myself that if these were only a few drops, they would dry out quickly and if not, well, I would take care of that when the time came.

Then there were more drops. I feared that all of a sudden these few drops would lead to a downpour. These few drops, falling quite intermittently, were keeping me from sleeping as effectively as if they had been part of a full-fledged shower.

What to do, get up or stay in the sleeping bag and try to get some more sleep? It wouldn't have done to get up. Not yet anyway; it wasn't raining. But those drops were beginning to drive somnolent me crazy. It loosely resembled Chinese water torture, now that I think of it. I longed so much for a couple of hours' more sleep and yet this idiotic drop, drop, drop kept me awake. I was psychologically ready to make a quick break to set up the tent. And yet it wouldn't quite let loose and rain so that I would be free from fearing that I had missed sleep.

And every time I drifted a little, ready to doze off again, there came the drops.

The bother over whether it was going to rain was beginning to outweigh any of the inconvenience a real shower might have caused.

At the next series of drops, overcome with irritation and wanting to put an end to this waiting in the quickest way possible, I threw off the top of the sleeping bag, stuck my head out and saw, with a fair degree of surprise, the precise source of my problem.

Birds.

As I travelled south from the forested area to the lightly-covered area to the plains again the water went from extraordinarily good to acrid in taste to impossible to drink. This was my experience at three wells at least, and at the last of these three the water had so much iron that the ground below was a rusty colour. The taste was so bad and strong that even the stand-by remedy of the orange mix did not mask it. So rather than drink it, the only alternative was to do without.

The road south from Swan River and Dauphin goes through the little town of Neepawa, about three thousand population. Whatever else this town is known for, it is also the hometown of Margaret Laurence, whose book, *The Diviners*, won the Governor General's Award for fiction. In a number of her fictional works, Neepawa is portrayed as the fictional Manawaka, Manitoba, a town that is as strait-laced as 1890 and, as some of those towns do, looked quite askance at anyone who deviated from the norm. After having read some of Margaret Laurence's things, I was curious to see the town.

It has a busy aspect from the west, with the usual edge of town businesses lining the road. The two roads coming into town are the Yellowhead Highway from the west and Highway 5, the one I had taken, from the north.

The main street of Neepawa is to the left as you go on the highway through the town. And as you turn north there, you can see ahead that the town ends quite abruptly, a more distinct cut-off than on the west side, and the farms begin again.

My first impulse was to go to a bookstore to look at the selection and see which of Margaret Laurence's books were in stock. Well, there wasn't a bookstore in Neepawa. What served as an outlet for books was a rack each in two drugstores. And these were loaded with the American fare that the large distributors put there. So the only recourse appeared to be the public library.

This municipal institution is housed in a small building on one of the side streets.

The clientele was a little older than I would have thought. The librarian, however was a lady in her forties. She had an excellent recall for the books that were in the library, especially the popular ones. She also knew the tastes of most of the users of the library. There's nothing like a small town.

My inquiry about Margaret Laurence brought a smile to her face. I realized that an often-spoken-about subject had been broached. She mentioned that there was a certain amount of sentiment against this author in her hometown. Part of it was due to occasional disparaging references to Neepawa. And part was due to that eternal bugaboo. For it seems, dear reader, that sex rears its head rather frequently in Margaret Laurence's work (as it does in life, — and Neepawa — for that matter). And because of this, a woman who is one of Canada's best-known authors is persona non grata in some quarters in Neepawa, and fairly influential quarters they be. This is, of course, akin to the many other situations in which an author has painted a picture of his hometown with a less than conciliatory brush. It happened to Sinclair Lewis when his fictional picture of Sauk Centre, Minnesota in *Main Street* caused him to be excoriated by the good citizens of that town for many years afterward. Then Sinclair Lewis won the Nobel Prize for Literature and you can guess the rest. Today a tremendous billboard invites the traveller to stop in Sauk Centre and see the original Main Street.

So Neepawa and Margaret Laurence have a similar relationship. A few of her older books are found in the Canadian section of the library. At a recent festival of the arts in Neepawa, the literature section was given to a discussion of the works of Nellie McClung, a Manitoba author whose work, I'm sorry to say, I haven't read.

The librarian told me that there was a whole gamut of books that she does not put on the shelf for fear of inciting or antagonizing some of the patrons. She keeps these books under the counter. That's the first time I've heard of purveying something "under the counter" at a library. The lady's spirit was admirable, though, and I hope that this revelation neither puts her in a bad position nor endangers the clandestine but licit traffic in books at the Neepawa Public Library.

Torn between riding along the Yellowhead Highway on a diagonal down toward Winnipeg and going directly down to the Trans-Canada Highway, I opted for the cut-off to the Trans-Canada because the Yellowhead Highway was heavily-travelled and, with no paved shoulders, it would have been a misery to ride on. And besides, the back road to the Trans-Canada Highway held the same fascination back roads always have.

The Trans-Canada Highway in this part of Manitoba had paved shoulders. This eliminates the danger from the cars, or at least from all but the wildest. However, the highway itself is like a conveyor belt, moving a steady and cacophonous stream of traffic from the east to the west and back again. That steady noise itself is almost debilitating. What I said before about the Trans-Canada Highway merits reiteration: It is a busy, noisy route and there are far more interesting things to see and do on the other roads that cross the country. Hitch-hikers and motorists seem to be afflicted with the same syndrome: they leave from the east (or west) and want to get to the other end of the country not caring, or perhaps not deigning, to see anything in between. It's a fast hurry-up-and-take-it-easy sort of vacation. They might as well take a plane. Some of the people biking along the road have the same attitude. They, of all people, should refuse to put up with the steady stream of traffic that only the Trans-Canada Highway carries. And they also sometimes share the attitudes of other travellers — fast is best. Don't take time to savour Ontario and the prairies. Keep your head down and go straight ahead. Don't take time to enjoy things. It is a pity that people have to be in a hurry on a vehicle that only averages 15 miles per hour. I often rode fast for short periods to get better exercise. But on the whole, the schedule was not a hurried one. I did not follow the Trans-Canada Highway all the way because of its being the shortest route between east and west.

I slept along the highway there and woke to a good tailwind the next day. And with that wind, it wasn't more than five and a half hours before I was in Winnipeg, a distance of about one hundred miles. Needless to say, this was one of the aforementioned bursts of exercise.

It didn't take long to cross Winnipeg, fortunately, for I had hoped to avoid cities completely. The only reason I had come to Winnipeg at all was to see Louis Riel's grave at St. Boniface Cathedral. There isn't much that attracts attention at Riel's grave. It is remarkable by its unobtrusiveness, hardly distinguished from the many other graves around except by its simplicity. It says simply "Riel" and below "1885". Near by there's a sign: "Riel, Président du Gouvernement Provisoire". In the west, it is plain to see how much Riel meant to the Indians; he was their symbol of hope. In going farther east, it is also easy to see that he is a great figurehead for the French as well.

Only a flat tire would have kept me longer in Winnipeg. This is not to criticize the city but rather its size.

There was a four-lane highway going east of the city. It was now the only choice I had. The selection of alternate routes to and through Ontario was nil.

I left Winnipeg with a large storm bank about fifteen miles behind me. This distance was quickly being shortened. It looked from a distance not like a shower but like a terrific downpour. I rode faster and faster, hoping that I would reach a restaurant or other shelter before the storm reached me. Stops of any sort were fairly scarce around here. It was never the rain that was intimidating but rather the chance of being knocked off the bicycle by a bolt of lightning was something to be missed.

I continued down the highway, casting intermittent glances to the left and slightly to the rear as I went. I had been doing this for some time when the thought occurred to me to look directly back down the highway in view of the feeling I had that the clouds were getting close. No sooner did I do this than I saw a tremendous wall of water bearing down on me from about three-fourths of a mile distant. The cars emerging from this water had their lights on. It was only after they left this great opaque curtain that I was able to see them. My speed shot up right away and the bicycle must have taken on the semblance, from the side, of an eggbeater. The front edge of the water hit just as I turned off on a little road leading to a country store. I was quite wet, although not yet soaked, by the time I entered the store.

I spent the night some twenty-five miles farther down the road after having waited out the downpour in the store. Traffic in this area had been especially difficult. The Trans-Canada Highway at this point was four lanes wide. But there were no paved shoulders — less than adequate gravel shoulders — and the traffic was very heavy because it was a Sunday, so much so that the highway was actually crowded.

The tent-spot-to-be that night had evidently been a picnic ground. The area had been cleared, there were lone trees standing on the grounds and car paths throughout. But whatever had been there — picnic tables or trash barrels — all was gone now and it seemed like a good place to stay.

This was one of those places with a great surplus of mosquitoes. Rain was coming, the mosquitoes were biting and I was in a hurry to get the tent up. Looking to set it up in an area open to the wind, I pitched it on loose earth. It didn't seem to help with the mosquitoes; they were incredible, perhaps the worst thus far. Setting up the tent while being attacked by mosquitoes was always more irritating because of the shorts and tee-shirt I usually wore at the end of a day's riding.

Had I the time to slip into long pants and put on a long-sleeve shirt, it would have been much less painful to put up the tent. However, changing into these clothes would have given these mosquitoes too good a chance at the real me. So I generally chose to suffer with the shorts until the tent was up.

It was normal to look down the leg and see four or five mosquitoes digging in for a drink, then to slap them one by one and quickly get back to setting up the tent.

Here I was in for it. The tent was up about ten minutes when the wind and rain came up. The tent was set up perpendicular to the wind so that the rain wouldn't enter the front or back flaps which were open. Unfortunately, this arrangement also offered more resistance to the wind. And the wind came up just after the rain did. It quickly tore out the stakes that hadn't taken solidly enough in the loose earth and the wet tent was upon me. There I was, all of a sudden, in a position of considerable vulnerability. It is amazing what security that tent offered when it was up, just like a cocoon. It was a protected island in a sea of rampaging elements.

I quickly crawled out and put the stakes in — deep

this time. The tent was wet but all was protected and no wind entered.

Traffic continued unabated the next day but the situation as a whole took a turn for the worse when the four-lane highway ended. Managing with all that traffic on a two-lane highway with lousy shoulders was next to impossible. There is a certain type of animal abroad on the highway. He is the one who is in such a hurry to get where he's going that he's willing to risk his life and everyone else's in the process, including he who is certainly the most vulnerable —the fellow on the bicycle. Some of the near misses are unbelievable. Four inches is certainly not too much clearance to ask and yet this is all that some deign to give. The car that passes the cyclist and nearly misses the oncoming car does, or could do, everyone a disservice; he could get them killed. And you know who would be faulted on the accident form. The fellow on the bicycle. Not the jokers who hadn't the time to break slightly from seventy miles an hour.

For a short stretch before the Ontario-Manitoba border, it began to look as though the wisest thing would have been to travel at night, such were the hazards of highway travel at this point. But then at the Whiteshell Provincial Park near the border, I saw that the traffic was, in great part, a kind of commuter group going back and forth from the park to Winnipeg. It was Sunday, after all. Once past the park where the siphoning off of traffic occurred, things were infinitely more tolerable although still hectic.

Paved shoulders even made an appearance for the last few miles to the Ontario border.

Part Three

Chapter 14

There at the border was a spiffy little tourist information booth run by the province of Manitoba. It was there I got a map of Ontario, which is doing things a little backwards in view of the sponsors of the information centre. Not only that, they served coffee on the house.

Taking it easy a bit in the tourist centre for a few minutes, a rather scruffy-looking fellow passed me on his way to the toilet. Now tourists are generally in neat order and hitch-hikers don't look as fatigued as this fellow looked. A little deduction on my part told me that if I looked outside, I'd probably find a bicycle. Such was the case.

He was called Pierre, a good Québécois from Montréal and on his way there. We struck up a conversation and then an association; we were to continue the alliance for several hundred miles.

Pierre had come east via Banff and Jasper National Parks after having left Edmonton. He too praised the virtues of travelling on roads other than the Trans-Canada Highway. He had gone north to Saskatoon before returning south to the Trans-Canada.

Pierre was of a droll cast of mind and this was to be an asset many times in later days when only a sense of humour could alleviate some of the impossible conditions.

We stayed that evening outside of a youth hostel east of Kenora. It was the first youth hostel I had seen since

Victoria and I still felt that there was nothing missed. I slept outside in the tent.

The following two days were uneventful. It was good to be riding with someone. Conversation passes the time and the miles.

The second day late in the evening we rode along in the dark looking in futility for a place to camp. We were about 80 miles east of Dryden, Ontario. By luck, we saw a sign in the dark indicating a private lodge. In we rode a half mile to find a great grouping of log buildings situated by the side of a lake. There was a camping area for tents, and although neither of us was especially fond of camping areas, we were won over by the especially warm looking log lodge, in which we could pass a comfortable few hours reading before the fireplace. The campground was not at all crowded.

This was another of the perquisites that do wonders for the morale. To be able to sit back in front of a fire with a book nearly erases the problems of the day and recharges the batteries for the next day.

I had the strangest sleep, or non-sleep, that night that I had had for weeks. I had taken a shower using shampoo for soap. I returned to the tent and not long after getting in the sleeping bag, I began to feel a biting rash. It was as if my arms were burning. As I touched my face accidently from time to time, the rash seemed to spread there. It was impossible to sleep under these conditions. And I tried to figure out what had caused it. The ostensible reason of course was the shampoo, although it was hard to see why something marketed as a shampoo would induce a rash so easily. Another possibility might have been the towel which I hadn't looked at too closely. Years ago I had an allergy to wool and this may well have been a recurrence of the same thing. The solution of this mystery, however, offered no relief for the night. There was nothing available as a recourse. The only possible way out of this imbroglio was to endure it.

Pierre seemed bothered also by this mysterious and torturous rash but it was hard to tell whether he was awake. I had no more than three hours' sleep that night.

By the first light next morning, the mystery was easily resolved. The painful rash-like feeling was caused, not by shampoo or a wool allergy, but by hundreds of no-see-ums biting in concert. They were impossible to see in the dark; they make no noise when flying around and it's hard not to have confidence in the tent's two screens, but the fearsome truth of the matter is that they offer virtually no protection against no-see-ums.

But we had had our showers and felt satisfied of that. We left the camp in good spirits, blissfully unaware that the next forty-eight hours would be one infrequently-interrupted shower.

It happened innocuously enough. We passed the widening of the road that is English River in a couple of hours. There remained a modest thirty miles to go to Uppsala, which to us then was only a brief stop we hoped to make early in the afternoon. The sky was dark but the clouds were hardly portentious. We covered about ten miles when I spotted some blueberries along the road. Pierre, who regularly rode slower than I did, suggested he go ahead while I attend to the blueberries.

It was a real trove. I had a good quart of succulent blueberries in twenty minutes' time. During this time, while my head was down and my eyes on the work, a formidable brace of storm clouds had time to move into the area.

After I had finished picking the berries and even taken my pleasure in eating them, I set off in the direction of Uppsala with twenty miles to go and a fair chance of catching Pierre en route. To my eternal chagrin, the rain hit like a twenty-pound sledge. Lightning began. The combination was enough to drive me to shelter. Shelter is, of course, a great exaggeration. What served as a slight defence against the rain, and hopefully a bit of protection against lightning — a frightful nemesis when on a bicycle — was a group of spruce trees whose tops formed a cluster. It was almost worthless as a shelter except for the small sense of security it gave. The downpour fell short of drenching everything; that is to say there were still some things in the saddlebags that were somewhat dry; I was wet through and through.

I made a break for it from the woods, hoping to get to Uppsala, fifteen miles away, before much more rain fell. I assumed Pierre had arrived in Uppsala already in view of the head start he had had. I envied him.

With hardly more than five miles on the road, the rain hit again. And this time it was no joke. I couldn't see worth a damn. The heavy rain, if I could have seen through it, was washing the salty perspiration into the eyes and it was stinging. Shoes, socks, shorts and shirt were all completely soaked. The wind was swirling and buffeting and making me cold. Suddenly the lightning crept up. The bolts were getting closer and closer. For a while, they held to one and two miles distant and then one by one they began striking closer. Needless to say, this did wonders for my speed. The bike was flying past the trees and I upon it was shooting glances back to check on the progress of the lightning.

Finally, when the rain was at its heaviest, and when it seemed as though the next bolt of lightning would surely have my name on it, I dove for the woods.

There is hardly any worse feeling than trying to take shelter when you've already been had. There I was, completely soaked along with everything I own — with the possible exception of a box of books in Montréal — and I was taking shelter. Standing under a couple of tall birches and a tamarack didn't keep any water away but at least the foliage cut the force of the wind and there was the feeling of being slightly out of the way of the lightning. This feeling may well have been misplaced; these trees on a little rise were probably the tallest in the area — I had been too much in a hurry to check. They undoubtedly could have guided the lightning right to me. It seems that an explosion occurs when lightning hits a tree. Of course, it would knock a lot of sense into whoever was standing near-by. (I'm lucky you're reading this at all).

Things were going from terrible to worse. The wind was mounting rapidly. The temperature seemed to drop and the rain increased. I was still in shorts and tee-shirt, freezing while waiting. It occurred to me that even a cold, wet long-sleeve shirt might keep the wind from having its full effect. So I pulled the shirt, completely soaked, from the bike and put it on. A little improvement. Then I got the sleeping bag, which had remained essentially dry until then, and unfolded the thing while retreating deeper in the woods. And then, of all the pitiful things I've been relating to you, faithful reader, I threw the bag over my head and crouched down under a leafy bush. I wonder if Jacques Cartier started like that.

I sat, finally, with the knees up against the chest, ensconced in a wet, malevolent world but feeling a measure of warmth and protection. It was actually a small step up from abject misery.

I must have remained under that wet shelter for an hour, wondering if anywhere in the world the sun shone. I regretted having picked the quart of blueberries and not having continued directly to Uppsala. But hindsight was an unusable commodity.

These are the times when having that special meal, a warm meal, becomes an obsession. Visions of fried chicken and mounds of boiled, buttered broccoli were the only diversion from the moment's misery. The only saving thought was that it wouldn't last.

All bad things should come to an end and this one did. I came out of my hiding spot in the last of the rain. I only wanted, somehow, to race the ten or twelve miles to Uppsala and find some way to dry out my things. Everything was soaked; it was only the tent that might have been useful. Worst of all was the sleeping bag; it was completely wet and those things don't dry quickly.

I froze on the way to Uppsala. My hands were as white as if it had been sub-freezing weather. The whole body shook with chills.

At last Uppsala came into view. It was going to be interesting to see how I would get out of this wet mess.

I learned soon that there wasn't a dryer in the settlement. One avenue was closed. The hotel there — nothing too chic — charged fourteen dollars a night.

It appeared as though Pierre had been spurred on by the rain. He had to have arrived in the village some time before I did, undoubtedly having beaten the rain. Someone at a local store said he had seen a fellow on a bicycle travelling through not long before. It seemed as though Pierre hadn't had the sense to wait for me and must have ridden on, still nursing the hope that he could out-ride the rain. There was no way I would catch him; it was too important that I dry the sleeping bag and a few of the other things.

I began, feebly, in front of the general store by wringing out the tee-shirt and the socks I was wearing. It was a start.

Then I looked up to see Pierre walking insouciantly down the road toward the store.

Pierre, as it happened, had had a very fortuitous break on our behalf. He had indeed arrived in Uppsala earlier but not before getting soaked by the rain himself. He did the most direct and reasonable thing he could have done under the circumstances; he knocked on the door of a house.

The first house he came to was actually a converted train station that served as a home away from home for two section hands who were working for the Canadian Pacific Railway. They were happy to have him spend the night there and to dry out his things. Pierre spent the intervening time drying out his clothes and changing into dry ones.

When he saw me pull into the village sometime later, he came to announce the good news.

It may not have been the most pleasant night I spent on the trip, but its conveniences were the most appreciated.

The rain didn't let up much the following morning but we both felt like going on. We could have hitch-hiked with the bikes but it wasn't a hitch-hiking trip we were making. As long as there was a reasonable possibility of making it by bike, we had to explore that possibility.

It does seem that rain does wonders for forward progress. Rapid pedaling is one way to try to build some warmth. We covered sixty or seventy miles in a few hours amid continuous rain, an annoying amount of traffic and a liberal sprinkling of fairly ambitious hills. We passed through Thunder Bay, bought some food and travelled north along the Lake Superior shore for a few miles until we came to an ideal camping place — a cleared off picnic area right near the lake.

Lake Superior must be the most magnificent of all lakes. Of the lakes that are called fresh-water lakes, it is the largest. It has a depth of over 1300 feet. The water in Lake Superior is so pure (and cold) that you can drink out of it nearly anywhere. Because its elevation is higher than that of Lake Michigan and much higher than Lakes Erie and Ontario, the pollution that is killing some of the other lakes does not reach Lake Superior. Lake Superior, however, has a major indigenous polluter. And that is the Reserve Mining Company in Silver Bay, Minnesota.

Some years ago the iron ore in the Mesabi Range in Minnesota began diminishing in quality. The ore that was being mined was less rich in iron than it had been. Then a process was developed to melt the ore down into pellets called taconite. This sort of pre-refining procedure cut down on transportation costs.

At the Reserve Mining plant in Silver Bay, the residue

from the taconite processing is washed into Lake Superior, sixty thousand tons a day. In the lake, it results in a suspension of material that blocks sunlight to life forms in lower strata of the lake. The currents in Lake Superior flow counter-clockwise. Duluth, Minnesota, not far from Silver Bay, has had to install a water treatment plant for the first time in its history to deal with the problem of purification that is a direct result of the negligence of Reserve Mining. This new water treatment plant costs six million dollars. It has been suggested that the problem could be alleviated as well with a few hundred pounds of dynamite.

We drank from the lake though and the water was good. Later that evening as the wind died down and the water calmed, the full moon rose over the lake.

The town of Nipigon on the north end of Lake Superior was to be an important point. It was a mail drop for me, a half-way point on the way to Newfoundland and a long-awaited farewell to the Trans-Canada Highway. The whole trip for the last several hundred miles had had to be made while dodging traffic all the time.

Pierre and I arrived in Nipigon in mid-afternoon and spent the next few hours having a beer or two and going through the mail.

Nipigon is a picturesque village situated between the Trans-Canada Highway and Nipigon Bay, an extension of Lake Superior. It sustains itself from commercial fishing on Lake Superior, the tourist industry and a few other service businesses. The main activity in the town appeared to be walking and driving along the streets, the common pastime in small towns everywhere.

We treated ourselves to a good meal that evening and then someone else treated us to a show at the only theatre in town. It happened very fortuitously. We were passing the theatre wondering if the budgets would allow a little diversion and looking at what was on the schedule. The owner spotted us and engaged us in a little conversation about our trip. At the end of the conversation, we were in possession of a pass to that evening's movie.

A change of pace, if it's a change toward the favourable, was always welcome. The movie was a strange affair; there were a number of apparently supernatural aspects and it was effectively done. It threatened to disturb our sleep. We spent the night on an out-of-the-way section of beach.

Nipigon got both of our votes as the best village of the many we had seen up to that point. Its setting was picturesque, its inhabitants friendly and the respite we got there was a long time coming.

Fortune smiled at us the next day and we looked the other way. We met a couple of French-speaking girls during the course of the day and had a limited picnic with them. But we left Nipigon, in accordance with our best judgment but against our hearts. We left Nipigon in the late afternoon, hoping to get to the shore of Lake Nipigon before nightfall. A junction half a mile east of Nipigon introduced us to the long-awaited Highway 11 and the escape from the Trans-Canada. We were finally relieved of the constant and dangerous traffic that had tormented us for so long.

By taking this route, we were to miss, among other things, the near legendary village of Wawa farther east along Lake Superior. The town had earned the reputation of being the most difficult place in North America from which to hitch-hike. Many who have passed through have stories of having spent an entire day in Wawa before getting a ride. There is even a story (from a newspaper report) of the fellow who spent twenty-eight days in Wawa without getting a ride. He met a girl there, married her and is evidently at the moment still in town. Whether he would still accept a ride out of Wawa is not known.

Highway 11 was the immediate change we knew it would be. Gone was the maddening traffic of the last six hundred miles. It is nearly sacrilegious to call that sort of thing bicycling. It is a test of the resistance of the senses to constant bombardment.

Now we rode north toward Lake Nipigon. This lake had always held a fascination for me and I had yet to see it. Lake Nipigon is big; one hundred miles across in places. It was part of the great canoe route from Lake Superior, up the Nipigon River and through the lake and then down to Hudson Bay. My early interest and cursory notice of the lake dated from a children's story I had read while young. It may have exemplified a certain romanticism.

The story was of a little Indian boy who lived next to a river north of Lake Nipigon. During the winter, the father sought to occupy his son by having him carve a canoe. This he did and when he had finished he had a small canoe that resembled his father's. In the canoe an Indian sat. The little boy carved his name on the bottom of the canoe and under that the words "Lake Nipigon". At the spring run-off, he lay the canoe on a snowbank. When the snow melted, the canoe ran down to the creek flowing by their camp. From the stream it flowed into the river that fed Lake Nipigon. Because of the length and number of islands in the lake, it took several months to cross. Finally, the little canoe was pulled into the outlet which is the Nipigon River. After having reached Lake Superior, it followed the currents to the ports of the lake, including Duluth and Superior. By a series of lucky events and not without accident, the little canoe from Lake Nipigon found its way through the Great Lakes and down the St. Lawrence to the Atlantic. A long time later, the little Indian boy and his father were in Thunder Bay and the boy wandered down to the docks. He was passing two seamen when he heard them reading from a newspaper. They were reading an article about a little canoe that was found by a ship in the Atlantic. And on the bottom of the canoe was carved the boy's name and below that the words "Lake Nipigon."

It's a nice story that sort of adds an aura of the faraway to the lake. There aren't any villages on the lake, which is a good sign in itself.

We passed north toward the lake along the Nipigon River. For the first time in a long time, since British Columbia and Prince Albert National Park I think, I began taking water from streams.

The villages again took on their own sweet provincialism, not unaffected by the passing tourist trade but neither controlled by it, as had been so many of the little towns along the Trans-Canada Highway. The first village we came to, Beardmore, was like this.

The businesses in these little towns exist to serve the local people for the most part. There's an openness because of it. If moose and bear hunting is a big activity in Canada, there's no doubt that it's open season on tourists all year around. Witness the difference in the little villages along the Trans-Canada Highway. In the smallest village, gasoline and food are clearly more expensive in the stations and restaurants along the highway than in the businesses just down the main street. Less a problem of supply and more one of avarice.

We came to the handy store of Beardmore. It had everything including books, a lunch counter, groceries and a good part of a drugstore. The proprietor was of French origin, although we didn't realize it for a little while.

"Are you French?" I asked.

"From time to time," he said, a little cynically.

"Depending on the customers?"

"Depending on the customers."

He was a jovial type who tried to sell Pierre nearly half the store. I evidently didn't look as vulnerable. Pierre had a sweet tooth that could barely be appeased. I think he bought two pounds of chocolate there.

Chapter 15

It was a pleasant nine-mile ride from Beardmore to the lake over a narrow and rolling paved road. We camped on the eastern shore of Lake Nipigon that evening. Our treat for the night was a fire on the shore and roasted marshmallows. Once again a case of small pleasures going a long way.

Pierre and I had been talking about the possibility of going two hundred miles in a day. I had done it on the prairies and the idea now interested Pierre. Neither he nor I believed in going too fast for fear of missing too much, but that mark was something special and a challenge. Beside that, it would be good exercise. (Sort of a coals-to-Newcastle approach, I admit.)

The gods were with us. Winds blew off Lake Nipigon at not less than forty miles an hour. The ten bellied out like an overfull sausage. Ça s'annonçait bien, as Pierre said. We fairly jumped on the bicycles, loathe to waste a moment standing on the ground when glory was only fifteen hours from our grasp.

We left as if pursued by the entire mosquito population of Ontario. It was only ten miles later that we stopped for our first food, whose character I can't recall at the moment but I do know it was taken when sitting by a spring. The spring was purity itself. We were sitting right by the three foot pool made immediately by the water as it left the ground. And you could see the little stream of water as it surfaced.

But this breakfast lasted only ten minutes. We were on our way right away.

I find it wonderful to concentrate while on a bicycle. If the speed is brisk and the road good, you can keep the wheels straight and your motion becomes an hypnotic experience. I wonder if anyone has ever been hypnotized by watching the movement of the roadway past the steadily turning wheels. Of course it is a good time for daydreaming. The bike stays on the road but the mind wanders and before long your thoughts are as far from this road as your imagination can take them.

We progressed well on this road. Number 11 is infinitely better than the Trans-Canada Highway, grace principally to the greatly diminished traffic. It was fun to ride together and to be able to talk. It was a welcome change from travelling single file with the head down and the ear tuned to the traffic approaching from the rear, hoping that your luck will continue and hoping that the next enraged semi-truck driver who passes won't be the last. I believe that sailing in a boat across the Atlantic or Pacific takes more courage and mental stamina than crossing the continent by bike. If that is true, then it is also true that a long bicycle trip is more dangerous than a long sailing trip and requires a greater expenditure of calories. It is more dangerous because of the animals lurking about the roads of the country, the unpredictable homo sapiens behind the wheel.

There are many reactions to a person on a bicycle, a number of which have already been mentioned. Several of these are unfavourable, unfortunately. I regret to say that my experience seems to suggest that the greatest number of near misses seem to occur between the heavy truck driver and the bicyclist. The majority of truck drivers are quite kind, but there is a certain number of drivers who seem to feel insulted that a person on bike has the affrontery to lay claim to a part of their road. These idiots pass within a foot, not content to give the man on bicycle a reasonable three or four feet of clearance. To these exceptions, I wish every form of bad luck. To the considerate men behind the wheels of the trucks of the nation, many thanks. One of the most irritating of simpletons is the moron who honks when he is just abreast of you. He thinks it's cute. Then there is the fellow who honks from well ahead or well behind you. He wants to get your attention so he can wave. This exchange of greetings on the road was one of the good parts of the trip.

There is another sort of driver who is a danger to everyone, and this is really unfortunate because he is the man who wants to give you all the room he can when passing. This gentleman frequently misses ending in a pile of junk only by inches. He almost always misjudges the speed of approaching cars. He may avoid running into another car (doing seventy miles an hour also) by only inches. It is too bad that this kindness could so quickly turn out the wrong way.

Pierre and I were covering territory rapidly. We arrived in Longlac in four and a half hours. I think it was 76 miles. In front of us was a long stretch — 132 miles to Hearst. This little bit of road would make a solid two hundred miles for us.

Just leaving Longlac we were drenched by a shower. It was cold and miserable. It didn't last more than thirty minutes but by that time we were entirely soaked. The sky was clouding up. It looked as though we would have thundershowers before evening. Rain would stand in the way of a 200-mile day. Farther from Longlac — 40 or 50 miles — rain was coming on our heels. This was a heavy rain and would certainly give us a hard time, maybe even a little lightning. When it was no more than a mile behind us, I told Pierre we'd better get in the tent or we'd regret it. He felt the same.

We laid the bicycles near the shoulder and put up the tent just as the worst of the rain started. We were inside and sheltered as the heaviest rain hit. It didn't last as long as we expected so instead of the satisfaction of having avoided a torrential and long-lasting rain, all we got out of the interlude was a wet tent.

That area was not particularly remarkable. About the only interesting features of the topography were some beautiful rivers that flow north to James Bay and Hudson Bay — that and an abundance of blueberries. Except for that, the area is weak in wood cover, being muskeg for the most part. In an area of muskeg, the conifers look stunted so the region as a whole was not too memorable. Fortunately, the traffic was light.

Nearing seven o'clock in the evening, the clouds appeared ominous. It was going to rain for sure and this time the rain looked like it would last. We had almost one hundred and forty miles that evening and any stop would mean the end of any chance to do two hundred miles.

We came to a lodge built of logs just as the rain caught us. The reluctant consensus was that we camp there and feel good about having done a good day's riding. The warm and welcoming aspect of the main lodge, built of logs, may just have influenced us a little in favour of staying.

It was disappointing to have to give up the goal of two hundred miles, especially in view of the fact that our trip is not a race and we rarely allowed ourselves a chance to see how many miles we could do in a day. Maybe another time.

Our anticlimax the next day was Hearst, which was to have been the end of our two hundred miles.

I wasn't able to find out if Hearst took its name from William Randolph but I assumed so. The lumbering industry is the sustenance of the area; most Canadian newsprint goes to the United States and Hearst's chain of newspapers was rather formidable, although I don't remember how great. Evidently Timmins was named after an American mining luminary.

In this area of northern Ontario, one sees the raw material from which nationalism is spawned. There are the mining and lumbering industries, for example. These were controlled for many years — they are still — by American companies. International Nickel has a large mine in Sudbury, Ontario. Because of the discharge from its mines' chimneys, there is a defoliated area of seven hundred square miles surrounding Sudbury. A trip through the area is an education. An encapsulated lesson in ecology and international avarice.

Sawmills line Highway 11 from Geraldton to Cochrane. The traditional métier of the Québécois has been that of the lumberjack. For that reason, the whole region is principally French, and from thence comes the second conflict. (The first, as suggested above, is the foreign control of Canadian resources and industry.)

The French in this area are required to submerge their culture to English predominance. This doesn't occur by fiat but rather by the intangible pressures that foist assimilation on sub-cultures throughout the continent. It would be possible, for example, to travel the whole distance of Highway 11, and to do so without realizing that the area is seventy to eighty per cent of French origin. This is because the road signs are not in French nor are the great majority of signs in towns. It is not until you get into the smallest villages that the signs are in French for the most part. Pretty small matter, you say? You must be English-speaking. The English-speaking ethnocentric majority on this continent has always assimilated the minorities. This may be understandable when it's a question of immigrants arriving in small numbers and filtering throughout the country. But when indigenous minorities, like the Indians or Eskimos, or minorities closely associated with geographic areas, as the French are with

132

Québec, when the minorities are washed away in the great wave of Anglo-Saxon assimilation, then it becomes especially lamentable. You see it beginning in Ontario as you move toward Québec. In fact it is more pronounced, perhaps due to the absence of the de jure protection offered by the government of Québec.

Here are some of the things that occur: (keep in mind that it is rather difficult to empathize with the minority at first if you have been enjoying the perquisites of the majority) First, there is the matter of language. This remains the most obvious. There are few road signs and few business signs in French. Pierre and I spent a whole evening in a restaurant located in a village of about two thousand. The village was more than ninety-five per cent of French origin. We eavesdropped in one way or another on conversations between more than forty people during the course of the evening. We heard not a word of English. And yet the restaurant menu was in English, the restaurant had an English name and every sign in the place, from the soft drink sign to the special of the day, was in English. The owners were French. It is very hard to seize this feeling if you are English-speaking. Whites undoubtedly didn't feel too inconvenienced twenty years ago in the U.S. South when confronted with a "whites only" sign at a drinking fountain. The problem is somewhat the same here: to accept the other man on equal terms and, occasionally, his terms. To some extent the problem is linguistic.

Some years ago I was speaking to an English-speaking man in Montreal about this problem. He was a well-educated man, a university professor, who had lived in Montreal much of his life. His French was not bad at all but he considered that some of the great worry of the Québécois for his language was exaggerated. He found it especially irritating that the Québec government should want to enact laws obliging certain groups to attend school in French,

"This is a free country and those who want to learn French are quite able to do it without government pressure," he insisted.

Does it happen often, I wanted to know.

"Sure; my wife and I speak French," he said, and it was evident.

"Some of our best friends are French." Does it have a familiar ring?

"They come over all the time?"

"Sure."

"And you go out to dinner or a movie together?"

"All the time."

"And you pass the whole evening in French?"

"Well . . . no. They all speak English."

It's indicative.

Hearst, for some reason, is a headquarters for five motorcycle gangs. What induces anyone to organize a motorcycle gang, here or anywhere else for that matter, is beyond me. There are about ten members in each gang. We never met any though.

Pierre and I stayed a whole evening in a restaurant in Mattice before camping there. One of the inducements for doing so was to pay court to a couple of young French ladies there. I am sorry to report that our combined charms did not have much effect, I might even say a reverse effect, but such are the vagaries of the road. This trip hadn't been much for romance; a good internship for one hoping to enter the priesthood I would think.

About twenty miles west of Kapuskasing, Pierre had a few problems with the bicycle, two broken spokes. Pierre had none to use for replacement. Now this isn't to suggest that Pierre be accused of any lack of preparedness. He was very well-prepared — but that was about six spokes ago. Pierre proved to me once and for all that buying an expensive bicycle, having an excellent knowledge of bicycle engineering and being well-stocked with spare parts is the worst conceivable preparation one can have before leaving on a bicycle trip. Something is bound to go wrong. For Pierre, things went wrong early and his bad luck continued unabated. From Edmonton via Jasper to the Québec-Ontario border, Pierre had ten flat tires and eight broken spokes. The back bracket on his bike broke at the bottom, his crank loosened in the one hundred thirty mile stretch between Longlac and Hearst and he hadn't the wrench necessary to fix it, the strap on his front handlebar pouch broke and, for good measure, his canteen bracket came off. The only thing Pierre had brought along which enabled him to deal at all with the repeated crises was a sense of humour. One day he may well establish a Canadian record, not in miles covered but in breakdowns and repairs. He had done his part for the economic well-being of innumerable bicycle repair shops across the prairies.

I have a suspicion that expensive bicycles are produced to earn a good profit, not in the sale of new bicycles, but by sales of replacement parts. Sort of like razors and blades.

If Pierre had sparing luck with his bicycle, at least he was lucky in repairing it. We stopped to replace the spokes at a small grocery store. Pierre's replacement spokes were too short and so his only chance was to find a bicycle shop in Kapuskasing. There were two women standing across the road from us and the little store, and they were waiting for the bus, as luck would have it.

We carried the disassembled bike across the road just in time for him to get the bus. He was on his way to Kapuskasing.

Buses accept bicycles as baggage without extra payment beyond the price of a passenger ticket. I have been told that airplanes do the same. I believe that bicycles also cross without charge on ferries, with the exception of a few in Québec.

Pierre's nostalgia for Québec was mounting as we got

nearer and nearer to the province. His songs increased in number, and their tone, now lugubrious, now joyful, reflected the haste he had. To leave Québec is to die a little, he said. He looked for songs in French in the jukeboxes along the way. His special lament in Ontario is the beer situation. There is a greater choice in Québec, the beer is sold in grocery stores and there is a special beer, a strong one, that will transport him and make biking a pleasure if anything will.

I must say though that our luck with the ladies took a turn for the better that evening.

We pulled into a village between Kapuskasing and Cochrane for the sort of extended relaxed evening that we so enjoyed savouring. Ordinarily the attractiveness of the girl has a tendency to increase in direct proportion to the time spent on the road. This wasn't the case here; the girls were truly beautiful. If rain kept us off the road, if a scorchingly hot day caused us to remain as long as possible under the cool roof of a bar, be assured faithful reader, that two young ladies can wreak havoc with a well-laid-out itinerary. The last thirty miles of the day are forgotten, the extra sleep doesn't count, the evening is young and the body and spirit in fine form. The lure of the chase wins over all.

What more is there to say except that the moon shone full that evening, the aurora borealis danced and swept the sky like celestial curtains. I had less sleep and more fun than any other night during the trip. This journey would have taken a hell of a lot more time with more nights like that one.

The next morning we left on four hours' sleep. Pierre's pace increased as we neared the Québec border. He was interested in no further diversions until we reached the magic line. Québec awaited on his horizon like a promised land. Accordingly, we went past Cochrane with only a brief stop of a couple of hours. Another stop around suppertime found us in a little hotel in Matheson south of Cochrane. While Pierre was off looking for a food store, I got in a conversation with a local old-timer. I tell you of this conversation because it was not untypical of the many I had with the local people en route. It went something like this:

Old-timer: "Going by bicycle, eh? Where ya comin' from?"

D.G: "Victoria, British Columbia."

Old-timer: "Pretty far, son! You live there, eh?"

D.G: "No, I live in Québec."

Old-timer: "Then what were you doin' in Victoria?"

D.G: "I went there to begin this bicycle trip."

Old-timer: "I lived in Victoria for a while. You like livin' there?"

D.G: "I don't live there. I live in Québec."

Old-timer: "You'll like Québec. It's good country."

D.G: "I know. I live there."

Chapter 16

Pierre and I took Ontario 101 to the east; no towns or anything were along the route but it was the shortest way to Québec. We had to assuage Pierre's spiritual hunger. Besides, the traffic was lighter on this road as compared to the more heavily-travelled route that went south through Rouyn and Val d'Or. A woman in Matheson reassured us that the road to the border was flat. She must have gone by helicopter her last time over the route. There were hills, lousy pavement and bugs. We didn't succeed in reaching Québec that evening but camped about twenty-five miles from the border. Pierre managed to break a spoke just before nightfall and as usual, this wasn't an ordinary repair job. The spoke that was broken was on the gear side of the rear wheel. Because of this, he felt he could fix it only at a bicycle shop in Rouyn. But he and the bicycle hobbled on.

This was a hilly country but muskeg was everywhere. There isn't much of redeeming worth in muskeg country; the trees are often stunted and the lakes dirty. Blueberries don't grow well unless the forest floor is somewhat firm and dry.

The road fitted in well with the muskeg. It was chewed up and overly-granular and bumpy. Long stretches were under construction. But we pushed toward the Québec border and the exhilaration that comes automatically on entering a new province on bike.

We had been riding for a long time it seemed and then the two signs came into view, the back of the Ontario sign and, on our side, the sign announcing Québec. The manner in which the road signs announce your entry into the several provinces is not only interesting but indicative of more than the simple passing of a political boundary. The sign for Québec is especially impactful. In other provinces, the border signs may offer a suitably benign message. "Saskatchewan Welcomes You." "Have a Nice Stay in British Columbia." But at the first sight of the Québec sign, the beat of the heart quickens and a perceptible shiver passes down the back. There against a bright emerald background and under a row of brilliant fleur-de-lys is one word — QUEBEC. And it's as if to say, "Now you're here."

Pierre's pace quickened as we crossed the border, the corners of his mouth drew apart in a contented smile and I couldn't swear to it, but I think I noticed a tear or two in his eye, although it may only have been a little salty perspiration dripping down. And for a while we shared that exhilaration that comes from having crossed into another province.

It struck us not long after entering Québec that it was hot, incredibly hot. A usual hot day was perhaps 30° C but this was something special. We had been without water for many hours. My being without water was my own fault. Some twenty miles before the border we had come to a spring, and seeing a spring after many miles on a bicycle means just slightly less than it would to a man lost in the desert.

We walked the forty feet back into the woods to the spring. The water flowed out of a pipe stuck into the ground. I put my hand into the water and it was ice cold. That was five or ten minutes already that I had been salivating at the thought of the water. So I did the natural but imprudent thing; I emptied my half-full canteen of the water of the day before, which was by this time of course quite warm, although soft and sweet-tasting. No sooner had I done this than I saw where the water was spilling the deep maroon colouring that is the sign of iron in the water.

I told Pierre that we wouldn't be drinking that water. We were both disappointed. I took a mouthful of it from the canteen and spit it out at the telltale egg taste. Pierre took some and nearly choked on it. I promised myself always to try new water before emptying the old.

We looked everywhere, rivers and lakes, for more water but much of it was murky. It felt like the temperature was approaching 35° C. We weren't getting very close to dehydration but it felt like it, and that's what counts.

After the border, we met a trucker who assured us that there was a restaurant only three miles away. Well what was three miles by truck was ten miles by actual measure on bicycle. Those things have a way of turning out like that. We found the restaurant finally though and spent a good twenty minutes satisfying our thirst with a variety of liquids. The next goal for Pierre was Duparquet where there was certain to be a grocery store. Québec grocery stores had an added significance for Pierre because they are allowed to sell beer, an integral part of his travel planning. Pierre's trip through Québec promised to be a hopscotch from one grocery store to the next.

After the obligatory stop at the grocery store in Duparquet for some beer, we were drawn to the hotel across the street by a desire to get out of the heat.

It was just after mid-day. We had heard several times already that it was over 36° C. Pierre and I had decided to end our long (in miles) and felicitous association. His bike needed repairing and Rouyn was the only place where it could be done. Then too he wanted to return to

Montréal while I was going to Senneterre and Chibougamau. What better way to have a final few laughs than over a beer in a cool tavern.

Our last few hours were pleasant ones. The stories we laughed over were lubricated with sufficient libation to get us through the heat of day. Pierre was especially effulgent, ordering one beer after another in rapid succession. He was home in Québec at last and soon would make a final turn toward Montreal.

We talked and joked and the time passed. It was as if we no longer wanted to go outside to face the heat. Along with the heat weighing against our going outside was added another factor, the comely innkeeper's daughter, or maybe I should say the innkeeper's comely daughter (can't be too careful about grammar). She would have altered the course of any man's trip anywhere.

Finally the time for Pierre's leaving came. He finished his last beer, we shook hands and wished each other bon voyage and he was off. The effect of the afternoon's beer had taken its toll on Pierre. He rode off shakily, just missing a telephone pole and negotiating the first hundred yards half on, half off the pavement.

I returned inside the tavern and whiled away the afternoon writing, more reluctant to go than Pierre was. Besides my attention was being drawn more and more to the innkeeper's daughter. She had short cropped black hair, light-coloured features and dreamy, faraway eyes. (Funny how a few beers and many miles on the road will improve any woman's looks.) She was tall, five feet eight inches I would guess, and this added to her classic appearance as she strode gracefully from table to table. (This last passage well illustrates why I'm writing non-fiction instead of fiction.) After some more beer and more and greater tips than my budget could reasonably be expected to absorb, I made a move. She was getting off at eight and yes, she wouldn't mind doing something after that.

Suffice it to say that we went swimming at a lake nearby and that the evening progressed from there. Anyone planning a similar trip should know that like encounters are wont to occur from time to time and should be anticipated in the time schedule. As an unexpected diversion from the itinerary, these are not unpleasant diversions, certain ranking ahead of getting drunk, picking blueberries or repairing a flat tire.

I put out the sleeping bag not long before the sun rose. The bugs were nowhere to be seen so there was no need to put up the tent. All the better, as I was treated to several examples of celestial phenomona. First, there were the Northern Lights which were fading out. Then two artificial earth satellites passed over, one not long after the other. And during all this time, maybe an hour and a half, there were six meteorites. They must have been part of a charted meteor shower, but I didn't have any idea which one.

Québec is an intriguing place for a lot of reasons, many of them linguistic. The French of Québec differs from the French of France because of, among a great many other things, the borrowing it has done from the neighbouring English. Hot dog is generally taken into the language as is, although the purists in the province may change it to chien chaud. Further confusion occurs with a hot dog stimé (steamed). Purists don't have much luck with hamburger, so that generally retains its spelling although not long ago on the road I saw it rendered hambegeur. This is due less, I think, to someone's trying to purify the language than to the likelihood that he was unable to remember the spelling in English.

Gasoline in Québec is simply gas, following the example of English North America. The Frenchman from France would rarely see a sign for essence, the word he is used to.

There are differences in pronunciation that would start a Frenchman crying on his copy of *Le Bon Usage*. Icitte (here) is often used in the hinterland for *ici*, *frette* (cold) for *froid*, *drette* (straight) for *droit* and the pronouns *moé* and *toé* are often used for *moi* (me) and *toi* (you). And if it's raining, you may hear *il mouille* instead of *il pleut*. But it's not much more complicated than this and involves only a little practice to get used to it.

A favourite reason offered by English-speaking people for not learning Québécois French is that it doesn't measure up to the French of France. When they want to learn *real* French, the *correct* French (so the story goes), they will go to France. In general, this appears to be a rather pathetic excuse for their own inability to learn French. It is as if the English spoken in the United States and Canada were not of high enough quality for a stranger wishing to learn English, that he had to go to England instead. Unfortunately, this attitude vis-à-vis Québécois French is rather common, especially in English-speaking areas of Québec. Montréal, for example, has an English-speaking population of 600,000, not ten percent of whom would be capable of holding down a job in French. A natural ethnocentrism on the part of the English and a few exigencies of the marketplace conspire to put the Québécois in a linguistically, if not socially, inferior position. It is pretty hard for the English-speaking person to appreciate the problem. It has been hard traditionally for the majority to empathize with the minority.

This sort of treatment is a slap in the face to every Québécois and they are beginning to realize it.

Québec recently enacted a law known as Bill 22. This law requires that all non-English-speaking immigrants to Québec attend French schools. The law has the English-speaking population of Québec in a dither, even though the law does not affect their children. It is characterized as fascist. In a de facto way, the rest of Canada, with small exceptions, has forced English upon the French since the beginning of nationhood. This sort of bill seems necessary if Québec is to guard its cultural diversity.

This whole area of Québec, the northwest corner of the populated part of the province, is known as Abitibi, after the lake of the same name that straddles the Ontario-Québec boundary.

In some ways, it is a microcosm that reflects much of the rest of Québec. But settlement in the region occurred rather late and only in great magnitude at the beginning of the century.

Foreign money in the mines and the logging industry is the backbone of the region. Without it, there would be no Abitibi, for all practical purposes. The farming done in the region would not sustain as large a population.

What does account for the great hustle and bustle — and pollution — of cities like Val d'Or and Rouyn is the mining industry. In years past, gold was a main extraction. It is still mined here although rising wages caused many of the mines to close down, including the one in Duparquet. Elevated gold prices haven't changed the situation much. Now copper is the principal mineral taken.

The route from Duparquet to Amos to Senneterre was a quiet one with few villages along the lightly-travelled roads. I was again experiencing the lassitude that comes with having taken a few days off. I was past the three thousand mile mark and a new sort of fatigue was taking hold. It hadn't taken long to overcome the physical fatigue, maybe a week or two. It was easy now to travel all day and not feel saddle sore nor feel a stiffness in the legs the next day. What was beginning to show itself was a sort of battle fatigue. It wasn't that going far each day was difficult, it was the fact of going at all that was beginning to weigh upon me. Perhaps it was just the after effects of having taken a few days off. Another factor may have been the relative absence of interesting points along that section of the northern Abitibi.

Up until reaching Senneterre, I had been facing the problem of how to get to the Lac St. Jean country, about three hundred miles northeast. To go the southern route to Montréal and back up was out. Too much traffic. So for a long time I had been settled on taking the Canadian National passenger train that went between Senneterre and La Tuque, Québec, a distance of around two hundred and fifty miles. I had taken the train once before and was looking forward to it again. It was one of the trains that serve the wilderness areas of Canada. Where these trains go, they stop where the passenger wants or wherever someone flags them down. They are the only lines of communication for trappers, Indians and the many others who live in the wilderness. A trapper, for example, might get on in Senneterre with his gear and tell the conductor that he wanted to get off at a lake one hundred miles distant. Once there, the train stops long enough for the trapper to get himself and his gear off. A romantic way to travel.

I was looking forward to a little comfort and ease, a little warmth and civility. There was no problem of worrying about taking the bicycle all the way; although this trip required a physical commitment, it was assuredly not an athletic feat. Travelling by train, ferry or some other means from time to time is in order. The purpose was to see the land and the people, not to work out for the Tour de France. Those who make an athletic exercise out of it inevitably lose contact with the countryside.

After all this pleasant reverie of the train trip, a few tidbits of information turned my attention in another direction. The road to Chibougamau, which I had always assumed was largely gravel, was supposed to have been paved to a great extent. The map I had was four years old and any map I had ever seen had gravel roads to Chibougamau. But the Québec roads department had been on the job evidently and after much work the past three summers, no more than thirty miles of the two hundred and fifteen to Chibougamau was still in gravel. The idea was tempting. To me, as to many in this part of Canada, Chibougamau was synonomous with the North. You might send someone north to Chibougamau in the same sense you would send him on a slow boat to China. It was almost five hundred miles by road north of Montréal. If you wanted to go farther north than Chibougamau, you went by bush plane, canoe or dogsled.

It was decided. Reason and caution were thrown to the wind: the destination was Chibougamau.

Chapter 17

There was a problem I was going to have to face finally and it looked like the road to Chibougamau was going to be the place. My tires had been more faithful to me than any two women ever were. But they were beginning to show their age, especially the one in front. That they had traversed the greater breadth of the continent nearly defied belief. But the tread on the front tire was beginning to wear through and the undertread showed. There weren't any bicycle tires in Senneterre; I had a roll of electrician's tape so I was ready for what might turn out to be some ludicrous repair jobs. I left Senneterre with only hope and luck holding the tires together.

Things went rather poorly from the beginning. Not an hour out of Senneterre I had set the tent up in the woods when I was hit by a hell-bent-for-leather thunderstorm. Lightning lit up the tent like a light bulb. The lightning and thunder came at closer intervals. The almost simultaneous blows of lightning and thunder sent me deeper and deeper into the sleeping bag. I thought of all the people I had wronged and hoped that I would be given the time to right those wrongs. I conjured up all the pseudo-scientific reasons why lightning should not strike the tent and leave a Kentucky-fried cyclist in its wake. I wasn't the highest point around; there were the trees. CRACK!!! The tent was rayon and the poles were aluminum, not very good conductors. CRACK!!! But then they were wet. CRACK!!! In forty years in the bush, Grey Owl was never hit by lightning. CRACK!!! But he knew what he was doing. CRACK!!! I might be hit just because I was ignorant. CRACK!!! Most salient reason: I hadn't yet seen my thirtieth year. CRACK!!! CRACK!!! Stupid reason no doubt. Nothing to do but to dig in. Whoever heard of someone getting struck by lightning in a tent while balled up at the bottom of a sleeping bag. (It reminded me to wash my socks more often.) No, there would have been no dignity in such a death.

But we survive these impossible situations and that too passed. Not before a little misery that involved the location of the tent. I had placed it over a ditch a few inches wide and a couple of inches deep. When the great rain came, water collected in it and formed a puddle in the tent. An hour or so after the rain stopped, I was able to sponge the water from the tent. But it was the end of the storm that really mattered.

It took three days to get to Chibougamau. They were three boring days for the most part with hardly anything to relieve the monotony. There were only two villages of any size, Chapais and Lebel-sur-Quévillon. Worse still was the scarcity of lakes along the road. Nor was wildlife abundant. I didn't see bear, moose or deer — not so much as a skunk. It was an endless procession of forest.

At one point, I camped at a place in the woods that was about forty miles from the nearest human being. It was a solitary night. To accentuate the feeling of aloneness the wind had died down completely leaving everything deathly tranquil. It was a bizarre and eerie feeling. Nothing moved. Once dark, there was no sound of birds, crickets or any other being.

It is strange, our fear of the woods. Most people have it. And yet it is largely unjustified. Of course, getting lost would mean a quick end. But assuming you know where you are, there isn't much to worry about. Perhaps this fear comes from the fear of the unknown, and the forest represents that above all. The bears and wolves won't bother anyone and neither will any other animal around here, unless perhaps it's a rabid animal.

I just saw a cartoon that sums it up. A man is reading a newspaper on the beach as his wife prepares to go into the water. "Mabel," he says, "you'd better think twice about going in. Somebody was killed by a shark on this beach five years ago." The headline of the newspaper he is reading says: "Holiday traffic accidents leave 498 dead."

For supper that evening and then breakfast the next morning, my dessert was blueberries. They covered the ground there in greater profusion than I had yet seen them. In twenty minutes, I had as many as I could eat in a sitting. Some of the berries were huge, as big in diameter as a thumbnail.

This was logging country. From time to time, logging roads left the main road to go back to the camps. Here and there along the road were great stacks of logs waiting to be taken to the mill. French-Canadians are known for being lumberjacks. Wherever wood is cut, from Newfoundland to British Columbia to northern United States, French-Canadians make up the majority of lumberjacks in many camps.

Far from the nearest village and hidden from the road by the trees, I noticed what I thought were tents and not the camping sort. They seemed year-round tents and as I turned back I saw that there were Indians living in them. It was regrettable that I did not stop but my mind was in a moving mood and so I missed a chance to see the Indians. It looked as though they may just have been the closest examples one might find today of the Indians of other days.

As if to accentuate the separation of this whole northern section, it began raining a cold and forbidding rain as I came to within thirty miles of Chibougamau. It was as if this northern town wasn't to be reached by bike. I put on my heavy jacket which is not water-proof but at least keeps the warmth in. Socks and shoes became quickly drenched. The tan on my legs looked very cosmetic when wet. It was one of those times when the mind goes on automatic pilot — you think of other times and other places, for to be wholly conscious of all of this is to be truly miserable. These were the days that added the extra flavour to the food in the restaurants, that provided the delicate pleasure in reading for an hour, that made you relish the comfort and exquisite luxury of a warm and dry sleeping bag. Chibougamau just would not appear. I thought of the other time a couple of thousand miles back when the same feeling was engendered by the seeming disappearance of Medicine Hat, Alberta. Then it was a long, cold night. Here it was a cold, northern rain.

Then Chibougamau spread out before me beyond the crest of a hill, first appearing like an outsized logging camp with the prefabricated buildings on the near edge of town, then showing itself for the bustling little town it is as the downtown district came into view.

The town of Chibougamau is situated on low hills on the south side of the great lake of the same name. It looks as though it was constructed in the area cleared immediately after a logging crew had swept through; where the cut stops, not far from the circumference of the town site, the forest begins forthwith.

According to what I was able to gather, Chibougamau was settled by fits and starts after the turn of the twentieth century. The lack of continuity in its settlement was due to the rise and fall of the prices of minerals mined in the region and also to interruptions caused by the two World Wars. A road did not reach Chibougamau until the late 1940's.

My first action on arriving in Chibougamau was to make a beeline to the nearest restaurant, at which place I ordered my own cure-all for a soaked-to-the-bone wetness and the general malaise that accompanied it — a chicken dinner. A little treatment for the spirit before attending to corporal matters.

After having begun a conversation with a few of the people sitting around the restaurant, I found myself very tempted to capitalize on an intriguing suggestion made by one of them. That was that the jail would always remain as a last resort as a place to stay. I had rather been set on spending the night in the tent or in a hotel perhaps, but the longer this idea rattled around in my head, the more I thought how sad it would be not to give it a try and to have missed seeing what it was like.

When the hour grew late, I strode over to the local hoosegow, bicycle under arm, and introduced myself. It was a rather sheepish inquiry, much as if I had walked up to the Chibougamau Hilton (such an animal doesn't exist) with the same bicycle and had asked the same thing.

Yes, they had room, I was told, and they would be very happy to put me up. The officer in charge was very amenable, an altogether hospitable inn-keeper. It was a modern jail, I suppose, as jails go. It was located in the newly-built City Hall, where it occupied the basement. The officer in charge stood behind a rakish counter and behind him were the two-way radios, typewriters and other tools of his trade. He ran through the gamut of questions about the bicycle trip. He offered to put me up and said that I wouldn't need my sleeping bag. But the bag is always a sure thing so I brought it along.

We brought the bike through the door of the station and put it in a storage room. Then we returned to the counter and he took my name — just like signing in to any hotel. But then came a little twist. He asked me for my belt (something that doesn't happen at the Hilton). This measure was necessary to avoid any possibility of my hanging myself on the premises. I had two thousand miles by bicycle yet to cover. In view of this, the possibility of hanging myself as an alternative was not altogether to be discounted.

I went out for an hour for a cup of coffee and a relaxed reading of the paper. When I returned about eleven thirty, another man was on duty. He treated me as cordially as had the first.

The jail was not sumptuous of course, but it was clean and the bunk, benefitting from two sponge mattresses under the sleeping bag, was comfortable. The whole had an aspect of cold concrete, a discouragement, of course, to continued use of the accommodation. But there was no noise and the staff was rather in tune with the needs of the customers, a change from the frequently more plasticized environment in more expensive places.

The next day I changed the two tires. The undertread was beginning to show on each. But they had held quite well, all the way from Victoria to Chibougamau. Evidently I had jabbed the back tube when putting on the new tire. Once filled it seemed to be losing air little by little. It looked bad but it was holding as I left.

I was beginning to get bush psychosis, and I hadn't even been in the bush that long. Nor did I have a partner, unless the bike might have earned that title. It hadn't let me down and it wasn't a question of chicanery between the two of us; it was just that over two hundred miles of staring trees in the trunks was beginning to get to me. And the fabulously beautiful lakes that are all over this part of Québec do not frequently touch the road so that a monotony that could have been broken was not.

In as much as no game appeared in the area, about the only thing that sustained my interest at all was the blueberries. I have an undying, even maniacal, interest in blueberries. One day I'll take up their scientific study. They have a humble beauty, a beauty that is truly spectacular in its simplicity. I have seen bushes that were pulled to the ground with the heavy charge of the berries. There wasn't a berry on these bushes that wasn't ripe.

Many of the berries were as large as marbles. My affinity for this boreal fruit could easily have been carried too far. I can visualize the following scenario:

I am found by the side of the road flagrante delicto with regurgitated blueberries streaming from the mouth. They call an ambulance and rush me to the emergency room at the St. Félicien Hospital.

A nurse takes charge and a young resident arrives on the scene within a few minutes.

"What is it?" he asks, the question a result of his limited experience.

"An overdose, Doctor," the nurse replies, her face reflecting the gravity of the situation.

"Cocaine, speed?" he asks.

"No, Doctor," she answers sadly, as if wishing it were one of these two. "Blueberries."

"Blueberries," the doctor replies, now aware of the seriousness of the case.

There not being time to call a specialist, immediate emergency measures are taken. First, pumping of the stomach. But the heart stops along with the breathing and the doctor begins cardio-pulmonary resuscitation. Nothing. Several other things are tried, to no avail. Finally, the nurse tries a full-on-the-mouth kiss and for a time the electro-cardiograph shows a response but it doesn't last.

Then the doctor, realizing that he is in grave danger of losing the patient, requests one last measure.

"Give him some sugar and cream."

There were many miles of gravel on the road south from Chibougamau to Lac St. Jean. I didn't want to put the tires to the ultimate test so I rode to where the gravel began and hitched a ride with an amiable trucker going south. We got together to lift the overloaded bike from the ground to the neck of the trailer to the top of the load of scrap iron he was carrying.

Lac St. Jean is a great country, well-sequestered from

the rest of Québec and the rest of North America by the Laurentian Mountains to the west, east and south, and to the north by the wilderness. It's filled with interesting characters. The whole land seems almost a place of mystery now, so many and so variegated were the things I saw there.

One of the legends of bygone days was a man whose real name I've forgotten but who was known to everyone as Alexis le Trotteur (the Trotter). Alexis was peripatetic in the literal sense; he ran everywhere he went. It started when he was a child. Alexis' father was going by boat across Lac St. Jean and he wanted to go along. For whatever reason, Alexis had to stay behind. But resourceful Alexis ran around the lake — which must have been twenty-five or thirty miles — and he beat his father to the other side. Alexis never stopped running, it seems. Soon he became known as a man who would race anything at any time. He did often — and won. There is a book on Alexis le Trotteur. It purportedly demonstrates that he would have fared well in the Olympics of his time. He had a great innate athletic ability. But it was widely believed that Alexis wasn't quite in order in the head. Evidently his mental capacity didn't quite match his athletic prowess. He met his demise when, while racing a train across a trestle in the region, he came up second best. The mere mention of his name is enough to make any older person in the area come alive with memories. Each has his own favourite of Alexis le Trotteur's exploits.

The people of Lac St. Jean are a special lot. They are known often as les bleuets (blueberries) because of the amount of blueberries harvested in the Lac St. Jean region.

I made the turn at St. Félicien to go clockwise around the north shore of Lac St. Jean. What a change to be in the flat, fertile farmland of the lake with a village every few miles. It was nice to be able to see people again, to stop in a tavern for a beer from time to time, to buy a newspaper and to stop in the little stores to ask directions.

In Mistassini, just north of Dolbeau, there is an old Trappist monastery dating from the nineteenth century. I wanted to stay the night there if possible. I had once stayed at a Capuchin monastery elsewhere in Québec and found the experience quite enjoyable.

I rode up to the monastery door about eight in the evening. The monastery hid in a grove of trees about one hundred yards from the road. The monk in charge of keeping the door was just closing it as I rode up. He was about fifty, clad in a floor-length white robe with a black cloth that went around the neck and fell down the front. Would it be possible, I asked him, to spend the night? Surely, he answered and said something that intimated that anyone who wanted to pray and meditate was always welcome. The evening meditation began in ten minutes, I was told. He asked if I would like to bring the bicycle into the corridor. It was expected that I pray, but then I had had to give up the belt at the Chibougamau jail.

I don't mean to suggest in any way that the monks at the monastery were anything but friendly and welcoming. After the evening meditation, the monk in charge of the door and I had a long conversation until late in the evening.

The Trappists did not speak among themselves or to others until seven or eight years ago. Most of their time was spent in work and meditation. The population had diminished quite a bit in recent years due to attrition through deaths of the monks. In 1950, there were nearly seventy monks in the monastery. Now there were thirty. One of the finest libraries in the region was housed in the monastery. This monastery is closely linked to the one in Gethsemane, Kentucky where Thomas Merton lived. His books are in the Mistassini monastery and are read by many of the monks.

I was finally shown my room. The empty rooms evidently got that way by the decrease in the number of monks. The room I had was located off a high-ceilinged corridor. The ceiling in the room I had was at least twelve feet high. There were two single beds with sparkling white linen and soft pillows the like of which I had only dreamed of. But best of all were the four foot high windows that opened to the garden. They were open all night, letting in the fragrant odor of the pine trees. Just under the window was a plain wooden desk with a little desk lamp. I sat at it and wrote for an hour. It felt good to be there.

Both morning and evening, I was invited to go to the dining room and to help myself to what I found. I had risen much later than the monks so I missed their morning meal. But I helped myself to the odds and ends from the refrigerator, including some direct-from-the-cow milk.

When I had thanked the monk in charge and said good-by, I went over to the chocolate factory that the monks run. The chocolate that they make there is sold in several other Trappist monasteries as well as to some local outlets. They had a variety, including white and dark chocolate and blueberry chocolate. This latter is supposed to be eaten within a few days lest fermentation set in.

Chapter 18

The little village of Peribonka about twenty miles outside of Mistassini has a history that far outweighs its size. It was there just after the turn of the century that Louis Hemon wrote the Québécois classic *Maria Chapdelaine*. I had read the book a couple of times and was looking forward to seeing the area.

I stopped at the little museum a couple of miles east of the village that houses some of the memorabilia associated with Hemon and the book. It was interesting to find out that the book had been published in over one thousand editions, that it had been translated into forty-five languages and that it had spawned three movies.

The museum itself, I'm sorry to say, seemed a little anticlimactic, as is often the case with these things. An author should be known by his work, as is just, rather than by the detritus he leaves. We risk being bored by the superfluities.

Maria Chapdelaine is a very evocative novel of Québec, although its occasional sentimentality may seem a little dated in our day. Hemon was from France and had just arrived in Canada. He wandered to Montréal and then to the Lac St. Jean country where he worked on a farm for six months. He was so impressed by Québec and the people who made it that he made it the subject of his novel. It is a story set around a romance that involves the heroine and three men, each of whom represents a part of Québec. One of them, the one she loves who later dies in the woods, is a romantic, lusty coureur-de-bois. Another is a farmer who works the day long like a horse just in order to clear his land, and to keep the forest from reclaiming it. The third is a Québécois who left the land, as did so many from the province, to work in the factories and mill towns of Massachusetts. In addition to the faithful evocations of habitant life drawn by Hemon, the reader is won by the raw charm of the people.

Hemon's *Maria Chapdelaine* is also a paean to the land and people. No better is this shown than in an interior monologue of Maria's at the time she has to opt for some kind of permanent station in her life. It goes something like this (faults of translation are mine):

"We came here three hundred years ago, and we remained . . . We brought our prayers and our songs from across the sea: they are still the same. We carried in our bosoms the heart of our people, valiant and alive, as quick to pity as to laugh, the most human of all human hearts: it hasn't changed. We marked off a new continent, from Gaspé to Montréal, from St. Jean d'Iberville to the Ungava, saying: here everything we brought with us, our faith, our language, our strengths and even our weaknesses — these are intangible and sacred things that will last forever.

"Foreigners have come among us . . . they have taken almost all the power, they have acquired almost all the money; but in the land of Québec nothing has changed. Nothing will change because we are caretakers — of ourselves and our destinies. We have understood only one duty: to persist . . . to survive. And we have survived, perhaps so that in several centuries the world will look at us and say: This is a race that will never die."

It is a book to read if you are interested in Québec.

Lac St. Jean and the country around it forms a kind of bowl. From the north side of the lake, I could see to the south rim as well as all the surrounding land. It was easy to see that the people were helped in their sense of homogeneity by the topography of the region. All of the cities and villages that surrounded the lake actually formed a colony.

I passed through the village of St. Henri-de-Taillon and wished that I could have stayed there for a few days — or a few years — it was so beautiful.

If it has not been previously clear in this narrative, he who rides a bicycle in the province of Québec taketh his life in his hands. There are far too many Québécois who, once behind the wheel, are like children with new toys. In my less restrained moments, I have wished that every man, woman and child of the province be locked up, only to be let out upon the successful passing of a driver's test.

The west end of Lac St. Jean, around Hébertville Station, was the home of one of the legendary strongmen of Québec.

Québec has a need of heroes. It makes heroes of the hockey stars. It makes heroes of the strongmen. It all adds to the homogeneity of the province.

Victor Delamarre died about twenty years ago. Yet he is spoken of in Lac St. Jean as if he were still alive. He was a man who weighed between one hundred fifty and one hundred sixty pounds, yet his strength was reputed to be greater than that of the great legendary strongman of Québec, Louis Cyr. Cyr himself was no lightweight. He owned a bar in the St. Henri section of Montréal. When a customer ordered a beer, his wife held it extended in her hand and Cyr in turn held his wife at the end of his arm.

Cyr was a giant, nearly three hundred pounds. Delamarre, at his lighter weight, once lifted three hundred pounds over his head with one hand. There is a photo of Delamarre lifting thirty-five Québec City policemen in a single backlift. An old-timer I met in another part of the province recalled meeting Delamarre as a child. Delamarre asked the boy for a quarter, bent it between his fingers and gave it back to him.

The Québécois like the spectacular in their heroes.

Lac St. Jean empties via the Saguenay River which in turn flows to the St. Lawrence. The Saguenay Valley had some of the first real hills I had seen since the Rockies.

A little impetus of some sort got me from the northeast end of Lac St. Jean to Tadoussac the same day.

Tadoussac, overlooking the meeting of the St. Lawrence and the Saguenay Rivers, traces its history back to the Jesuit missionaries of the early 1700's. Its location on the St. Lawrence is breathtaking.

From time to time, I satisfied an idiosyncratic taste of mine by having something to eat in an expensive restaurant. In this town it was the Hotel Tadoussac. It was much like the lavish Canadian Pacific hotels that stretch across the country. These visits of mine were never for full meals, only snacks or desserts. I linger over whatever I have and read a little, and my strange intermittent desire for something de luxe is largely satisfied.

I took the ferry from Les Escoumins across the St. Lawrence to Trois Pistoles. Thus doing, I added something to my knowledge of geography. Atlantic tides mount to this point, in fact well to the west, nearly to Québec City. So a large part of the St. Lawrence is salt water. Somewhere in my mind I had assumed it was fresh water to the northern tip of the Gaspé Peninsula.

But once on the other side, what a surprise! The incredible, almost tangible beauty of Gaspésie. Pictures never convey the real essence of special places. Gaspé is one of these places. The sinuous road as it sweeps up and over a hill and down to a bay where a village is nestled, the houses, some quaint some modern, others overwhelming in their antique beauty, the smell of the sea blown over the land, the shops selling fish and the stands selling homemade bread and doughnuts, it just doesn't exist elsewhere in Canada like this. The mountains, the prairies, the lake country — they all have their partisans. But it is hard to find a region with as many individually beautiful constituents as Gaspésie.

I stopped at Bic just outside of Rimouski after having left the ferry. I had a friend there, a young Gaspésien lady whom I had known for some time. I spent a couple of days with her family and began to feel more of Gaspé than an outsider would when passing through.

The house they lived in was nearly two hundred years old and built rather close to the road in the Québec style. It was solid; they were all solid in those days. Or maybe it is that we have no way of seeing the ones that weren't well built. This one was two storey, square and had been refinished inside. Part of the furnishings were pieces of furniture in wood that my friend's father had made. They were highly polished and quite ornamental. The mother was the picture of a French-Canadian housewife, stout, smiling, and author of a cuisine that could have kept me there for years.

A question of mine led later to a wonderful culinary find. I asked rhetorically what was meant by the Canadian food sign on so many restaurants throughout the country. Certainly it was a misnomer. All the common dishes that were served, hot dogs, hamburgers, French fries and the like although perhaps invented elsewhere, were certainly popularized in the United States. So where the Canadian food?

As the adjective Canadian in Québec nearly always means French-Canadian, my challenge was taken up and the next day the young lady and I went to lunch at the Ti-Québec, a restaurant in Rimouski. Located in a basement and decorated with Québécois scenes, it served principally dishes that were indigenous to the province.

I had a pot-au-feu and made a mental note to come back and try some of the other dishes one day.

What a great relaxing change it was from the road to sleep in a big old comfortable bed.

I think of the whole time of the trip up to Rimouski as the time B.C. This B.C. stands for Before the Crash. The crash was not a literal one but rather a nightmare that took the form of a number of flat tires. And a nightmare it truly was. I suppose it is ungrateful to complain. After all, had not the bike made it from British Columbia to Chibougamau without a hitch? Bad luck came in spades. It is almost painful to write about it.

Suffice it to say that all the problems centered around the back tire. It went flat and I repaired it. Then it repeated. The damn thing wouldn't hold air and I couldn't see what was wrong with it after having checked the tube, the tire, the tire rim and spokes. I hardly have the stomach to go on. After the new tube blew, I took my beloved infidel to a bicycle shop, a well-equipped one at that. I let the mécanicien à bicyclette know that we had a special problem on our hands. He tightened the spokes, balanced the wheel, straightened the axle and went over the rim with a file. Fifteen miles away from that shop, the tube again blew out. I went back to the shop again. And left again. And blew another tube. By this time I was down the road to Ste. Anne des Monts, well into Gaspésie, so I tried another bike shop. Keep in mind that after each of these flats, I ministered to the problem myself. Not that that was worth anything (obviously). All the same, it is not difficult to patch a bicycle tire. But I left Ste. Anne des Monts and it held. What a nightmare it had been, one that cost me several days.

The trip from Ste. Anne des Monts to Percé was remarkable for the absence of real problems. There was a stretch of hills after Mont St. Pierre that could have qualified as true problems however. They rose from sea level to an abrupt eleven hundred feet. There are certain walls I would have preferred to those hills.

It is only the road that brings any travellers to the north side of Gaspésie, there being no airports and no train service beyond Matane. Maybe some of the charm of the area is due to this.

Of the many things hawked as souvenirs throughout the continent, probably the best done are the four-masted schooners that they sell around the Gaspé Peninsula. They're made of wood by the many people who sell them along the road. The smartest of the shipmakers have their alluring daughters doing the selling. I am sorry that I didn't buy one but space was lacking.

I'll never forget Gaspésie. I think that perhaps it may have been the most beautiful of the many beautiful areas of the country. Every little bay revealed a picturesque fishing village nested below the great hills of the peninsula. Or the village would be perched on the hills high above the sea. The houses were of wood, nearly all white and had a solidity that suggested they would be around long after you and I.

The peninsula was dotted with lighthouses, some of them stationed high on cliffs above the sea, others way out on promontories jutting out into the water.

The wind changed to easterly as I came to the tip of the peninsula. And for some reason it remained a headwind until I got all the way to New Brunswick. For this to happen, it had to change all the way around, from an easterly to a westerly wind, as I rounded the Gaspé Peninsula. The days were often interrupted by showers. Road construction was quite frequent. As I remember them, these last three hundred miles of the peninsula were rather difficult.

At Percé, I made the mistake of staying in a youth hostel. This for the second or third time during the trip. There are doubtless many good youth hostels in the country. Unfortunately I have not seen many of them. I had the seeds of an addiction when I left on this trip and now that addiction had become deep-seated. That addiction was to fresh air. The hostel was filled with people smoking. All these people are against air pollution naturally (because the big companies do it). For them to be able to equate cigarette smoking with air pollution is as unlikely as their being able to equate energy with mass times the speed of light squared. They are all in the country where they wanted to be and they're hell bent on recreating the urban environment as soon as they can. Pollution in Montréal and Toronto was something they railed against so they came hundreds of miles to one of the most beautiful parts of North America, shut themselves tightly in a large room and proceeded to poison the air, not only for themselves but for others who never liked air pollution in any of its forms.

In a way, it's slightly analogous to a short story Jack London wrote. An American goes to a country in South America as the guest of a very aristocratic, supposedly civilized family. He quickly becomes enamored of the daughter, a young woman possessed of gentility and dignity such as he had never seen. The whole family goes to a bull fight. When the bull is being killed and the blood is running all over and the bull's flesh is hanging out, the whole family, including the graceful daughter, are screaming their hearts out for more blood. The American is so shocked that these supposedly refined people could be crying for the blood and death of this animal that he goes beserk.

So one day I'll write a story and the hero will be a hapless joker who leaves the city for a while to escape the air pollution and the constant bombardment by noise. He goes to an idyllic lake and ends up in a youth hostel. There he sits all evening amidst a myriad of practising guitar players and the occasional iconoclast who has a flute that he doesn't know how to play. And they're all sitting in a room whose poisoned air per cubic meter far exceeds that of any large city on the continent. And our poor hero goes beserk, or something appropriate.

Percé is spectacular for the several hundred foot high rock in the harbor that has become famous. The town itself is beautifully situated on great hills that give a view of the Percé rock and Bonaventure Island. Of all the places on the Gaspé Peninsula, it is this village that is the most touristic. But it is not bad considering that nearly all of the rest of Gaspésie is nearly unspoiled.

As I shifted from east to south to west rounding the tip of Gaspé, so did the wind change against me. Most of the trip down the south edge of the peninsula to New Brunswick was made against the wind with the odd cold rain. There was a little more traffic on this side of the peninsula but the great hills I had encountered on the other side were few and far between here. I felt that once finished with Gaspé another watershed would be passed and it wouldn't be far to Newfoundland.

The south part of Gaspé is inhabited by a great number of Irish and other English-speaking people. You would think they would learn French, sequestered as they are in faraway Gaspé, but it isn't too often the case.

I rode through New Carlisle, the birthplace of René Lévesque. It is ironic that the head of the separatist Parti Québécois should be born in a town with an English name and majority English population.

It took several days from the trip down from Percé to New Brunswick. I was able to cut off a few miles by taking a ferry across Chaleur Bay to Dalhousie.

Any form of travel was a nice change from the bicycle, especially a ship. I had been on the bicycle for over four thousand miles at that point. It's a pity that the ferry ride across to Dalhousie was only three miles. It could have gone to Newfoundland and I couldn't have been happier.

Part Four

Chapter 19

I harnessed a tail wind after Dalhousie going along Chaleur Bay on the New Brunswick coast. It felt good once again, like an old friend come back. It had been several hundred miles and many days since I had had the westerlies.

At first New Brunswick seemed English, as might have been expected. But as I rode south along the New Brunswick coast I noticed French in evidence here and there. It was usually the villages where the special character was most noticeable. Whole villages were French. The signs were in French just as in Québec. This was Acadia, made famous by Longfellow's *Evangeline*. Acadia was the old name of the French settlement in the Maritimes. There were towns and villages here before there even was a Canada.

The Acadians were in the Maritimes in the early eighteenth century. It was in 1755 that the great deportation of Acadians took place. Today in the French areas of New Brunswick, reference to "La Déportation" is not uncommon.

Nathaniel Hawthorne heard the story of Emmeline Labiche, the woman whose sad tale served as the basis for *Evangeline*. He in turn told Longfellow and suggested that it would make a good piece to write about.

It is very interesting to look at the generally-used English edition of *Evangeline*. It is quite provocative — that is, if you're Acadian. The edition is printed in the United States by a large paperback house. The cover blurb announces the poem as a moving tale of the strength of the American spirit, describing Evangeline's life-long search for her departed lover Gabriel. Well, Evangeline was Canadian, not American, if we take in mind the later political status of the region and assume America to be synonomous with the United States. Did they feel that as long as it was published in the United States that they could call Evangeline American?

The other bone of contention that could drive present-day Acadians up a wall is contained in supplementary material at the end of the book. A brief historical outline of the time is given. The gentleman who is assigned to give the historical facts surrounding the deportation attempts to prove that it was justified from the British perspective (read justified, period) because the British had to protect their territory against the French. This included therefore the several thousand Acadian peasants who would supposedly abet France in a possible conflagration. So they had to be deported, whether they wanted it or not and whatever the cost in human terms.

These two examples of attitudes in the American edition of *Evangeline* published in our day illustrate the cultural myopia which brought about the deportation over two hundred years ago.

Not all of the Acadians were taken south and not all of them remained there either. Traditionally, the first to return was Alexis Landry who came back within a year or two to Caraquet, on the cape that juts into Chaleur Bay east of Bathurst. His grave is in the cemetery there.

One of the nicest meetings I had during the trip occurred in this area. I stayed a couple of days with the retired parish priest of Grande Anse. Monsieur le Curé lived with his housekeeper, whom I came to know as Ma Tante Cécile, and her niece.

M. le Curé was a voluble character in his early seventies. He was thin, grey-haired and ever-ready to laugh. He was several years retired from his active duties as a priest although he still said Mass every day in his house. His retirement didn't keep his parishioners from calling him however. The two days I was there were filled with calls.

Once a lady called and she was quite distraught. It seemed that the local doctor, a much-loved man, had just died. Her only recourse was M. le Curé.

"What do you want me to do? I'm no doctor," he answered with his usual originality.

"Ah, but M. le Curé, you're so much better than a doctor," the woman pleaded.

M. le Curé's passion was his garden. And the focal point of the garden was the carrots, which represented a large portion of the vegetables produced. M. le Curé assured me that carrots were the very best vegetables one could get. Consequently, we had carrots at every meal. And when I finally left, I left with saddle bags full of carrots.

Unlike almost all the younger priests around, M. le Curé never went anywhere out of the house without his black garb and Roman collar. But around the house and in the garden, he wore no collar, had his shirt open down the front and this left open his long underwear underneath.

Ma Tante Cécile was a wonderful, ebullient woman with a great sense of humour. She was just short of sixty. Her passion was feeding men. And I was fed as if they didn't want me to leave, or as if I wouldn't be able to leave after having had one of Ma Tante Cécile's meals. Her apple pie was the stuff of which dreams are made.

At the noon meal on the last day I was there, she prepared a lobster, fried fish and all the trimmings. I was trying to figure out a way to take Tante Cécile along, perhaps a fully-equipped trailer, but no concrete plans materialized. The cuisine of Ma Tante Cécile was unforgettable.

M. le Curé and Ma Tante Cécile also felt the pains of being part of the Acadian minority. They said that when they went into a store in Bathurst, a town which is half French-speaking, English clerks could not serve them in French. It was they who were continually expected to accommodate the English. Likewise at a gathering of people, if there were nine who were French-speaking and one who was English-speaking, the conversation was in English.

I rode out the road past Grande Anse around the peninsula down to Chatham. This was the most solidly French area of New Brunswick, the south being the English-speaking descendants of the Loyalists who fled the Thirteen Colonies at the time of the American Revolution. The other parts of New Brunswick are generally mixtures.

I broke a couple of spokes north of Chatham. They were on the back tire on the side of the dérailleur gear so I had to take it in to a bike shop to be fixed.

The more frequent bike repairs and the time dragging on in general was giving me a case of the let's-get-it-finished-before-the-snow-flies fever. There had been too much dallying (and not a little dalliance). St. John's, Newfoundland was still a long way off. If I was to get there soon (this was around the first of September), I had to put some solid mileage on each day.

I camped the night just south of Chatham, New Brunswick. It was raining the next day. But I wanted to make up ground nevertheless. If it rained, I either stayed well-sheltered or got quite soaked. There was no middle ground. Either stay in the tent all day or ride and keep riding. It made no sense to ride for a while, get soaked and then stop somewhere to attempt to dry off. No, there would have been no future in that. So that day I rode all the way to the ferry for Prince Edward Island which crosses over at Cape Tormentine, New Brunswick. They were one hundred and ten very wet miles. I regretted not having more ferries to take.

Prince Edward Island is what the Royal Canadian Navy could adequately protect in the event of a major war. It is the smallest of the provinces and the least populated. I'm tempted to add my own two qualifications to the list. It just may be the most beautiful province. Of course, it is subjective in the extreme to say this. Each province has a beauty that appeals differently.

Prince Edward Island also may offer the most difficult bicycling of all the provinces. Surprised to hear me say this? Try it. There are more ups and downs per mile in Prince Edward Island than anywhere else. One lady in a country store on the island told me that the great majority of the tourists described the island as being flat. All I can say is give them a bicycle.

The hills are everywhere, on every lane and byway. They're not long but very steep and quite annoying. I sometimes wondered what effect this quick variance in terrain has on the system. It doesn't hurt it, certainly. It would be interesting to find out whether it develops the muscles and cardio-respiratory system as well as steady travelling. I tend to think it does a better job.

It was as if all the picturesque vales, all the neat white houses and all the pretty little country lanes had been gathered from all over Canada and placed on Prince Edward Island.

I went up toward Cavendish on the north side of the island. Where else can you bicycle from one side of the province to the other before breakfast?

I went up a hill, straining as I hadn't since Gaspé to climb it and then came sailing down, hair blowing in the gush of wind and wheels humming at the great speed. Then that road stopped after five miles and turned into another one which went three miles before turning off. The country was like a checkerboard of roads, much like the rural areas of England. The hay had already been cut and the apples were ripening. Cows grazed in the fields and made it resemble Wisconsin in pastoral beauty.

A fair number of people who have heard of Prince Edward Island have heard of it because of the children's classic *Anne of Green Gables* by Lucy Maude Montgomery. I believe that the book was published just after the turn of the century. It has been bringing tourists to Prince Edward Island ever since.

I had planned on visiting the area around Cavendish where *Anne of Green Gables* is set so I made a point of buying and reading the book before getting on the island. The book is a treat. A real children's classic. I found later that Mark Twain had called Anne the greatest creation of a child character since *Alice in Wonderland*.

Anne has a vivid imagination. That is almost an understatement. The book is an encomium to the imagination. To Anne the whole area around Cavendish is a wonderland of natural beauty. Her imaginings give a splendorous patina to everything. The book reminded me of what Baudelaire had said. "The imagination is the greatest of the faculties, because it alone understands the universal analogy." Quite a combination Baudelaire and Lucy Maude Montgomery, aren't they?

The area around Cavendish is well worth the visit, even if you have to do it by bicycle. This part of the island was especially well-sprinkled with the hills that people in automobiles don't believe exist.

Cavendish, and the whole island, is a charming place that comes close to being enchanted. The roads that cross the island connect with other roads every four or five miles so that the whole island is a criss-cross. If I had one month to spend on bicycle and had to spend it in one province, I believe I would do it in Prince Edward Island. And I wouldn't miss a mile of those country roads. I'd stop on purpose at every country general store and buy an apple or an ice cream cone and if the conversation warranted it, I would spend an afternoon in the store. These stores are probably the only ones in Canada that, in great numbers, so well fit the image of the old general store. In other parts of the country, the stores in the country often tend to be a tumble-down gas station and grocery store combination, just a nondescript grocery or the proliferate and super-efficient franchised gas station.

That's one reason why Prince Edward Island is so warm a place. It is said that in the summer, Prince Edward Island's population of 70,000 is doubled and even tripled with the influx of tourists. You would think that the people of the island would become superficial as a result. But this wasn't the experience I had. They were extremely warm, open and civilized. While I was on the western side of the island, I had to meet a mail drop across the island in Souris. It was a Friday and I wanted the mail before the week-end so I parked the bicycle six miles south of Cavendish (at New London in back of Lucy Maude Montgomery's birthplace) and thumbed rides to Souris. Prince Edward Island must be the best province in which to hitch-hike in Canada. In earlier years, I had covered every province at least two times on the thumb and that was the feeling I had then too. Prince Edward Island was amazing. When on the island about seven years ago, it took three rides to get where I was going. I had had only to stick my thumb out for four cars. Three of them stopped.

Going to Souris, the luck was almost as good. What a truly friendly province! I therefore saw the eastern part of the island not on bicycle but by thumb.

I hitched back to New London and arrived there in the late evening. Hitch-hiking is a fine way to travel. It is a very much demeaned mode of travel however. The common belief (held without any real examination of the problem) is that the practice is dangerous to driver and hitch-hiker alike. To the driver because many hitch-hikers are thought to be robbers and murderers. To the hitch-hiker because of the supposed numbers of pederasts behind the wheel. A wholly ludicrous assessment of the situation on both counts. But hitch-hikers, being young and frequently impecunious, are fit objects of this propaganda.

Some years ago, while passing through Minneapolis, I read an advertisement, a quarter page, that had been placed in the paper by the state association of automobile dealers. It carried dire warnings, without any substantiation, about picking up hitch-hikers. This below the photo of a fellow trying to get a ride on the highway. This is a bit ironic, because these same automobile dealers, through their manufactured-to-wear-out cars have been the perpetrators of more crime connected with highway travel than all the hitch-hikers on the continent.

There's a test you could try if you're interested in sniffing out the crime on the highway. Travel from Toronto or New York to Vancouver or San Francisco picking up every hitch-hiker you can along the way. On the return trip, stop in several service stations per day and tell the mechanic in charge that you think you have something wrong with your motor but you don't know what it is. (This works better if you're a woman.) Then find out what his estimate of the cost of repair is. You'll find out quickly from whom you'll be getting robbed on the highway.

It is always assumed that a woman hitch-hiking is letting herself in for rape. I had always had a tendency to believe this. But it may not be true after all. Last year they had a transit strike in Toronto which sent everyone to the street to hitch a ride. Before the strike, one and one half per cent of the rapes in the city occurred when the victims were hitch-hiking. During the strike, when greater numbers of women were hitch-hiking, the percentage of rapes related to hitch-hiking jumped to twelve per cent of the total. But — and this is an important but — the total number of rapes was the same during the strike as before the strike. Which suggests that a given number of rapes is likely to occur regardless of the circumstances, that rapists will find their prey independent of a specific locale or opportunity. In other words, that extra ten and one half per cent of women who were raped while hitch-hiking during the strike would have, had they not thumbed those rides, been raped while on their way back from the local supermarket or the other instances in which rape occurs. Hitch-hikers and hitch-hiking are easy targets because no one makes money from the practice.

In Poland, the government has instituted a system in which hitch-hikers obtain books of tickets to use while hitch-hiking. When the person is given a ride, he gives one of these tickets to the driver. The driver in turn redeems his tickets for prizes.

Not only is there no better place to hitch-hike, but there could hardly be a better place to visit than the lovely little island Camelot in the Gulf of St. Lawrence named after Prince Edward.

I camped a night near New London and rode on the next day to Charlottetown. It was a funny experience to ride over the hills and then arrive in the villages from a different direction, having already passed through on bicycle a few days before or on the thumb in the meantime. There was a crossroads in every village. And if you wanted, you could turn there and go up to the next village six miles along that road. You could continue that all day, which is a pleasant thought indeed. A far cry from getting bush psychosis on the road to Chibougamau.

Everything seemed to be on a smaller scale in Prince Edward Island. The University of Prince Edward Island has fourteen hundred students. I think the high school that I attended had more than that out for football. Charlottetown, the capital and largest city, has a population of under thirty thousand. A paragon for us all.

I cycled through the streets of Charlottetown to the Centennial Centre, which is a complex consisting of a library and museum.

When getting directions of some people, I was asked the usual questions about the bike and the attendant gear. When I told them I had come from British Columbia, they were amazed. And, funny thing, for the first time I thought about it a minute and *I* was amazed.

Surprise is the usual reaction when people learned that the bike trip had spanned the continent. The questions are predictable: How long has it taken? How many miles have you come? How far do you go in a day? Some of the people found it so incredible because they once rode twenty miles on a bicycle and were exhausted. (Between you and me, the first twenty miles are easily the hardest) I was sure that toward the end of the trip, after I had answered that I had come from British Columbia, someone was certain to say, "Can you prove it?" But it never happened.

Wood Islands is thirty-eight miles from Charlottetown and is the embarcation point for the ferry to Nova Scotia. I made a quick three-hour trip of it with rain hot on my heels. If it was going to rain, I wanted to be on that ferry when it did.

That ferry wasn't a bad bargain — seventy-five cents for the fourteen mile crossing for passenger and no charge for the bike.

In the summer, the line-ups for the ferry are enormous. It is not uncommon to wait twelve or thirteen hours for a ferry, such is the number of cars travelling through. That is one of the advantages of a bicycle; you would never have to wait but would simply ride to the head of the line.

I landed in Pictou after dark having ridden the four miles from the ferry landing in the dark, making my way by the feel of the route and intuition. I had only ridden at night three or four times during the trip. I had no light, not thinking that the infrequent use it would get would warrant it. Ordinarily, it would be no problem to ride at night; there is enough illumination, even without the moon, to see the road. The problem arises in a road filled with holes. A road which has a generally smooth surface can often have holes deep enough to cause a blow out or substantial enough to throw a rider from the bike. These things aren't difficult to spot by day but at night they're almost impossible. I was bedded down most evenings after sundown so I could avoid this particular hazard.

I had a nice dinner of fried clams and beer in a tavern in Pictou and then went just outside of town to set up the tent.

This whole part of the trip was under the continual threat of rain. It looked like I would be in the St. John's area at mid-September at the rate I was going. If rain hit and stayed, it could have sent this trip into October, and who knows what sort of weather is visited upon Newfoundland in October.

So I wanted to continue while the riding was good and the weather remained favourable. I wanted to keep to at least seventy miles a day. Less than that and I thought I'd see snow in Newfoundland.

I bicycled a good eighty miles the next day, from Pictou to the Canso Strait and Cape Breton. What a refreshing meeting awaited at Port Hastings. I met two girls on bicycle who, with two other girls who had gone off for a while, had bicycled all the way from Michigan to Cape Breton Island. Those four girls had travelled over two thousand miles together. The exercise had done them well; they were tanned and well-muscled. To listen to their stories was one of the best times I had on my trip.

They had bicycled through Michigan to Sault Ste. Marie and then had followed the Trans-Canada Highway past Ottawa. That alone is quite an achievement. The traffic along that two-lane highway is almost insufferable. But they seemed to have made it all right. They made frequent stops, which must have helped greatly. They began their day at six in the morning, rode easily all day and stopped at four in the afternoon. Their average day was fifty miles and they had done as much as ninety. When I met them after two thousand miles, they had been on the road for five weeks.

One of the girls worked in a hospital and joined the group after hearing her two friends discussing it. They left a few days later. That's the way these things should be done. Get up off the coccyx and get to it. To hell with weeks of planning or doing it next summer.

Their stories were pure entertainment. Especially the ones about the sleeping places. It seems that they frequently slept in churches. There is a church in nearly every village. They went up to the parsonage or rectory and asked politely if they might stay in the church for the night. Most of the time they were able to put their sleeping bags in the church and quite often they were invited to breakfast the next morning.

The enthusiasm those girls exuded was contagious. I felt as bright-eyed as I had when leaving Victoria. I envied all the domesticity that must have been attendant with their trip; warm and varied meals and clothes washed frequently. For a pittance I would have detoured and followed them to their horizons.

I made a quick crossing of Cape Breton, missing the Cabot Trail which may have been a hilly copy of Gaspé, missing also Cheticamp, the large French-speaking town along the Cabot Trail. And the many villages where Gaelic is still spoken. But I did go through Baddeck, the little town on Bras d'Or Lake where Alexander Graham Bell spent thirty summers. He said that other regions may have spectacular beauty but for simple beauty, no place surpasses Cape Breton.

I rode into North Sydney, getting into town about eight o'clock just ahead of some rain. After visiting some friends in Sydney Mines for an hour, I boarded the ferry for Port-aux-Basques (you can see that the pace was increasing toward the end of the trip). The ferry trip was a reasonable six dollars and a dollar and a half for the bicycle, which is not too bad for a one hundred mile trip.

Arriving by ferry into Port-aux-Basques has always been a strange experience for me. It's an eerie feeling. If the moon had wet seas instead of dry *mare* and you arrived on the moon by splashing down in the sea and then travelling by boat to the moonport at the edge of that sea, I think that that moonport would look like Port-aux-Basques.

There is an omni-present fog surrounding the town which sits in a little bay. Little vegetation is apparent so that the whole scene is one of rock and water. At no place I have visited have I felt such a true other-worldliness.

I hit Port-aux-Basques just after six in the morning. I hadn't slept more than a few hours so there was a choice between a few hours' sleep in the tent somewhere close or departure into the cold and driving rain that was the order of the day. With amazing disregard for the proper care of the bike as well as a like disregard for my own health and morale, I shot out into the rain.

It would have been possible to hope that a few hours' sleep would have outlasted the rain but only a fool would have believed that. I'll believe that it always rains in Port-aux-Basques until I see concrete proof to the contrary.

I stopped at a couple of gas stations on the edge of Port-aux-Basques to get a road map of Newfoundland. They were in short supply but I finally found one. A road map would probably not have been necessary. It's pretty hard to get lost where there's only one road. There are a few side roads on Newfoundland but only one that goes the whole way east to west. It's 565 miles long — a good healthy stint.

When I stopped for the road map, one local man said that I would probably see snow before reaching St.

John's. It wasn't hard to believe with the freezing rain that was falling at that moment.

I usually checked off a few points on the map as intermediate goals before I set off in the morning. This time I didn't. St. John's was too far away to think about and so were the towns in between. Nothing to do but put the head down and get to it.

I was thoroughly soaked before leaving the town limits of Port-aux-Basques, if it has a town limit (even if it hasn't). I had not a dry stitch on my body. I bet I was even getting water on the brain. In spite of this and in defiance of all logic, I felt that I was becoming wetter through fault of the water's being thrown up on my back by the rear wheel. Getting wetter is like getting more pregnant. That water thrown up by the rear wheel was making my morale wetter at least. It had to be stopped by some sort of fender. I found a little board by the side of the road and got off the bike to get it. I jammed it under the rear baggage rack, the operation being performed in the aforementioned cold downpour with water dripping profusely from my nose, ears and chin. It did stop the extra water on the back though.

To compound an already unfortunate situation, the winds were intense and their velocity was increasing. They were driving the rain so hard at me that I could scarcely see the road. Then I saw, just barely, an ominous warning. It began: "Warning, winds in this area have been known to attain a velocity of one hundred twenty miles per hour. If you should experience difficulty in controlling your vehicle, try to . . ." and then I lost it because I was too busy trying to control my vehicle.

If hell were wet and windy instead of hot, it would have looked like that forty-mile section north of Port-aux-Basques. I rode through the pass at the point where the Long Range Mountains meet the sea and the wind really increased. The mountains and the coastline formed a corridor through which the road passed. And the whole length of the corridor was swept by tremendous winds. The winds came up from the south coast of Newfoundland, hit the straight Long Range Mountains, spilled over them and swept down with a chinook-like effect.

I spit out the sweat that dribbled down into my mouth and it landed on the shoulder on the other side of the road. The wind increased again and I could not stay upright on the bike, much less control it. I got off to walk it, with barely more luck. My arms ached as I struggled to keep the bike, and myself, upright. After walking it for quite a while, I came to a place where trees bordered the road and this broke somewhat the great force of the wind, enabling me to get on the bike again.

By suppertime of the first day, I had reached St. Fintan's, a distance of about sixty miles — very good in view of the extreme conditions.

Rather than go on in the early evening, I stayed around a little restaurant there for a few hours.

Although it had stopped raining in the late afternoon, it rained again — hard — that night. I rather imprudently had pitched the tent in a little place that later became a puddle. So during the night, the water came across the floor of the tent and then into the sleeping bag. My tent had never let me down in the rain. This was my fault; a little foresight would have avoided the situation. The ladies in the restaurant told me that during the night there had been some very heavy lightning and thunder for a few hours. They had all been awake the full time. I must have been very fatigued from the day because I slept through the whole thing without noticing it; if I had awakened during the night and had seen the lightning and thunder, I certainly would have kept my own vigil too.

My second day on Newfoundland was no luckier than

the first. It rained a good part of the day and slowed my progress accordingly. I bought a big salted cod in Cornerbrook and kept that with me for sustenance. It kept well. Salted cod is a very salty proposition but a good chew.

It was moose season. I heard shots along the road from time to time. I half anticipated getting bagged myself. Would have made an interesting mount for some American's trophy room.

I rode the fifty-four miles from Deer Lake to Baie Verte junction with a nice tail wind, sun and dry weather. It was like the prairies. It felt good to open it up (who ever heard of "opening up" a bike) cover some ground fast and get some real exercise again.

There are many things in out-of-the-way areas that miss the passer-by's eye. I realized this again in Springdale when I picked up a copy of the local newspaper, a bi-monthly issue. The quality of writing in this newspaper was its own reward, transcending the import (or lack of it) of the news that was reported. The styles of the writers of this newspaper were in no way constrained by the strictures that limited the journalists writing in the Montréal Gazette, the Toronto Star, or the Vancouver Sun. They reported the news as they saw it in their own distinctive ways. The gentleman who reported the news from Lushes Bight on Long Island (an island not far from Springdale) was particularly interesting. I'll give you an excerpt of his news report. I have changed the names but have not tampered with the reportage in any other way.

"The Labor Day weekend brought a lot of visitors to Long Island for Lushes Bight. There were some just visiting and more just home to stay which we will hear about in this news.

"Visiting your correspondent over the Labor Day weekend was Mrs. Herman's sister and her husband, Byron Barrett and family and her nephew Ernest Barrett and wife and family, also Mrs. Herman's nephew Michael and Mrs. Brown and children and Michael's sister, Mabel Sparks and daughter and son from King's Point.

"Saturday evening when all the visitors came we got a surprise as our son Bert Herman and his wife Helen and William and Martha arrived home from Kitchener, Ontario where he has been working for almost two years. Bert is home to stay now. The same weekend the people of Lushes Bight had a short visit from a gentleman, Mr. Fred Noble from Vancouver, British Columbia.

"Your correspondent had a long-distance call from Triton from his half-sister, Mrs. Herbert Peebles of that place, only they are living at Triton for the summer months. She told me that her brother Eric and his half-sister, Mrs. Vernon Peebles and her husband from Triton would be up Sunday so they arrived Sunday dinner time after forty-five years. Mr. Noble has been here and he is seventy-six years old and his father, the late Matthew Noble has passed on since he was home last.

"Mr. Noble was born at Pilleys Island, which was his father's home. He was the oldest son of his father by his first wife. There were three brothers: Maxwell Noble, still living in Canada on the mainland and his youngest brother, Horace Noble of Miles Cove who was going to visit him Monday and I thought Mr. Noble said he never saw him. He can't remember him as Horace was taken to Miles Cove when his mother died when a baby and was brought up by the late Mr. and Mrs. Robert Foley of that place."

It seemed to me during my crossing that Newfoundland was the province most unlike the others, save perhaps Québec. It was due to many things; the language, the home-grown journalism of which you've just had an example, the fishing villages numbering over a hundred that have no roads of any sort and also the many colourful names on Newfoundland. Look on any map of the island and you'll see them. Come-by-Chance (the only way to travel), Lushes Bight (rather suggestive), Heart's

Delight, Heart's Content, Joe Batt's Arm (part of Joe is immortalized at least), Blow Me Down and Happy Adventure.

When I was on Newfoundland several years ago, I experienced something that I've been wondering about since. There were occasions — many of them — in which I had difficulty understanding the local speech. In the intervening time, I had asked myself often whether it were really possible that spoken English had been so difficult for me to understand. I speak a couple of languages other than English and have reached a point in both where repeating is seldom necessary. Could it have been true that people speaking English — my own language — were forced to repeat what they said several times so that I might understand?

Well it was. I listened often to people speaking, especially older persons, for long intervals without being able to understand what was being said. Often younger people were just as incomprehensible to me. It seems to result from a faster speech coupled with a slightly different intonation.

The road was in good condition and fairly level all the way to Gander. I was counting off the miles for the day when the trip would be finished. Each time I passed another hundred mile milestone, it reassured me that St. John's wasn't far away.

Just east of Gander I spent the night with a family whom I will long remember. They had thirteen children and because of the number, some had to sleep in a shack in back of the house. There was an extra bed in the shack and it was mine for the night. The shack smelled of I don't know what and was almost as cold as the tent would have been. I put my sleeping bag on top of the bed and slept in it rather than unfolding the bed clothes. Although they lived in a small community, the family had an outdoor toilet, a real pungent one, and got their water from a well just outside of the back door. I ate breakfast with them the next morning. They didn't have much but they gave me all they had. That's a better accounting than most of us could give.

It was getting cold in those final days and nights. I worked myself into all sorts of creative positions inside the sleeping bag in order to keep warm. In the late afternoon and early morning, my hands froze white on the handlebars. Winter was making its approach felt. The first cold always hits hardest.

As I got closer day by day to St. John's, the incredible proposition of actually finishing began to occupy my thoughts. After it was over the fine physical conditioning would go and only the memories would be left. But those memories would remain a lifetime. The memories of the villages of the prairies, the lake country of Ontario, the remarkable breadth of this continent — five thousand miles, of idyllic, storyland Prince Edward Island, of the poetry of the Indian names — Capitachouane, Mistassini, Chicoutimi, the cuisine of Québec, meeting bears in the wild, the fishing villages of Gaspé, the overpowering solitude on the road to Chibougamau, the beautiful girls of Acadia, the days of rough cycling — ten hours to cover forty-one miles on the Hope-Princeton highway, of glorious riding — two hundred fifteen miles in a day, and special memories of three very impressive lakes — Kootenay in British Columbia, Kingsmere in Saskatchewan and the haunting beauty of the greatest lake — Superior.

The Avalon peninsula before St. John's was almost as mountainous as the Malahat Pass on Vancouver Island where I had passed almost four months before. Then on the last day I came up a steep hill, pumping hard, and pulled to a stop at a country store near the top of the hill. There was an old man, close to eighty, seated on a box in front of the store.

He watched me as I rode up to the store, then asked, "Where ye comin' from fella?"

I was still panting heavily and the best I could do was to gesture to the rear with my thumb.

"Where ye headed for?"

"St. John's," I managed to say, still breathless.

"St. John's!" he exclaimed. "That's thirty-seven miles!"

f

DISCARDED